"In a world dema
Dibbens-Wyatt (an
are loved as we are:
greatness but to seek Christ—and that practicing contemplation can sustain us on this countercultural task. My soul needs the quiet truth of this timeless and timely reminder."
—**CATHERINE McNIEL**, author of *All Shall Be Well* and coauthor of *Mid-Faith Crisis*

"I love reading Keren Dibbens-Wyatt's work."
—**RICHARD ROHR**, Franciscan friar and author of numerous books, including *The Universal Christ* and *The Wisdom Pattern*

"Julian of Norwich is one of most amazing, wise, and visionary Christian writers of the Middle Ages—or of any age. Her story of dealing with serious illness, confinement, and maintaining powerful optimism amid unimaginable suffering makes her a true spiritual teacher for all time. This deeply personal and richly contemplative book dialogues between Julian's wisdom and inspired reflections grounded in Keren Dibbens-Wyatt's profound spirituality and life, which echoes Julian's in some surprising ways. This blessing of a book is a beautiful example of the Spirit-infused riches that can come our way when we prayerfully engage with the wisdom of the great Christian mystics of the past."
—**CARL McCOLMAN**, author of *The New Big Book of Christian Mysticism* and *Eternal Heart*

"I have always been impressed by Keren Dibbens-Wyatt's strength and resilience in the face of chronic illness. *All That Is Made* took me on a journey into the life of Julian of Norwich and other mystics that helped me understand this resilience. Dibbens-Wyatt's life and book are anchored in a rich contemplative understanding that resonates with my soul. This inspiring book is a must-read for all who seek a deeper understanding of the spiritual life of contemplative prayer."
—**CHRISTINE SINE**, author of *The Gift of Wonder* and host of The Liturgical Rebels Podcast

"Into a contemporary world where so-called influencers are large and loud yet often lacking substance enters a book authored by a little-known Christian mystic living with chronic illness, focusing on an obscure

fourteenth-century woman who had visions, with a disarming emphasis on a tiny hazelnut. Careful readers will be invigorated by these compelling juxtapositions and struck by the power of fragility in nurturing genuine spiritual strength."
—**DR. ROD WILSON**, author, speaker, and consultant

"From the first pages of *All That Is Made*, when Keren Dibbens-Wyatt writes that she was curled up in God's heart like a seed, we know we're in the hands of a wise *evenchristen*, Julian of Norwich's word for a fellow believer. Dibbens-Wyatt's chronicle of how Julian walks beside her through chronic illness reminds us that no matter our situation, we 'can still be friends' with the one who created the moon and stars. When we gaze upon Christ and feel ourselves decreasing, God is actually returning us back to our eternal beloved self."
—**CHRISTIANA PETERSON**, author of *Awakened by Death* and *Mystics and Misfit*

"Reflecting powerfully and lyrically on Mother Julian's image of the 'little thing the size of a hazelnut,' Keren Dibbens-Wyatt shows us how profoundly we are cherished by a triune God who upholds and sustains all things. Biblically informed and joyfully creative, this is a text to savor and pray with. *All That Is Made* is a wonderful witness to 'the brightness and centrality of God that is everywhere.'"
—**SARAH LAW**, author of *Sketches from a Sunlit Heaven* and editor of *Amethyst Review: New Writing Engaging with the Sacred*

"A poignant tapestry of contemplative spirituality, grappling with life's mysteries through the lens of Julian of Norwich's hope-filled assertion, 'All will be well.' This beautifully crafted narrative invites readers to explore their own interior landscape, illuminated by the holy graces of Christian contemplation amid human sorrow and struggle."
—**WENDY MURRAY**, author of *Inner Healing the Franciscan Way*

"Keren Dibbens-Wyatt has given us a gift amid her suffering by sharing the comfort and wisdom that God has given her. I'd recommend this book to anyone who wants to draw near to God, no matter whether they are in a difficult life season."
—**ED CYZEWSKI**, author of *Flee, Be Silent, Pray* and *Reconnect*

All That Is Made

All That Is Made

The Comfort of Contemplative Prayer

Keren Dibbens-Wyatt

Harrisonburg, Virginia

PO Box 866, Harrisonburg, Virginia 22803
www.HeraldPress.com

Names: Dibbens-Wyatt, Keren, 1971- author
Title: All that is made : the comfort of contemplative prayer / Keren Dibbens-Wyatt.
Description: Harrisonburg, Virginia : Herald Press, [2025] | Includes bibliographical references.
Identifiers: LCCN 2025013523 (print) | LCCN 2025013524 (ebook) | ISBN 9781513816395 paperback | ISBN 9781513816418 ebook
Subjects: LCSH: Julian, of Norwich, 1343- | Julian, of Norwich, 1343- Revelations of divine love | Contemplation | Revelation | Love—Religious aspects—Christianity | Christian women—Religious life | Chronically ill—Religious life | Devotional exercises | BISAC: RELIGION / Christian Living / Spiritual Growth | RELIGION / Mysticism
Classification: LCC BV5091.C7 D53 (print) | LCC BV5091.C7 (ebook)
LC record available at https://lccn.loc.gov/2025013523
LC ebook record available at https://lccn.loc.gov/2025013524

Study guides are available for many Herald Press titles at www.HeraldPress.com.

ALL THAT IS MADE
© 2025 by Herald Press, Harrisonburg, Virginia 22802. 800-245-7894.
   All rights reserved.
Library of Congress Control Number: 2025013523
International Standard Book Number: 978-1-5138-1639-5 (paperback);
   978-1-5138-1641-8 (ebook)
Printed in United States of America
Cover and interior design by Merrill Miller

All rights reserved. This publication may not be reproduced, stored in a retrieval system, or transmitted in whole or in part, in any form, by any means, electronic, mechanical, photocopying, recording or otherwise without prior permission of the copyright owners.
   All scripture quotations, unless otherwise indicated, are taken from the Holy Bible, New International Version®, NIV®. Copyright © 1973, 1978, 1984, 2011 by Biblica, Inc.® Used by permission of Zondervan. All rights reserved worldwide. www.zondervan.com The "NIV" and "New International Version" are trademarks registered in the United States Patent and Trademark Office by Biblica, Inc.®
   Scripture quotations marked (ESV) are from the ESV® Bible (The Holy Bible, English Standard Version®), Copyright © 2001 by Crossway, a publishing ministry of Good News Publishers. Used by permission. All rights reserved.

29 28 27 26 25   10 9 8 7 6 5 4 3 2 1

For Rowan, always.

O God, I could be bounded in a nutshell, and count myself a king of infinite space, were it not that I have bad dreams.
—**WILLIAM SHAKESPEARE**, *Hamlet*, act 2, scene 2

To see a World in a Grain of Sand
And a Heaven in a Wild Flower
Hold Infinity in the palm of your hand
And Eternity in an hour
—**WILLIAM BLAKE**, *Auguries of Innocence*

Contents

Foreword • 13

1 Meeting Julian of Norwich • 17
2 My Journey into Contemplative Prayer • 25
3 Julian and the Small Round Thing • 37

God's Creation Is . . .
4 Small • 49
5 Fragile • 61
6 Round • 87

God's Children Are . . .
7 Made • 99
8 Kept • 109
9 Loved • 129

God Is . . .
10 Heavenly • 137
11 Holy • 149
12 Home • 157

Conclusion • 165
Julian's Prayer • 171
Acknowledgments • 173
Suggested Reading • 175
Notes • 177
The Author • 183

Foreword

My father was a doctor. Many nights at dinner, he would tell us about the day's patients. It was as if he were decompressing, processing with us the intensity of helping people in life-and-death situations. To be honest, as a boy, I wasn't always interested, and some of the details he shared didn't seem terribly appropriate for the dinner table. But looking back, I learned so much from him and his dinner-table reflections on his day.

One of the greatest lessons I learned was that proper diagnosis is essential to healing. It's only after a proper diagnosis that doctors can offer the right prescription.

I believe that Keren Dibbens-Wyatt's new book is the perfect prescription for three kinds of people. You may be one of them!

First, you may be a spiritual seeker, whether you are religious or not. You are always looking for "something more" in life. You don't want to simply skim over the surface—you want to experience the deeper dimensions of this amazing gift of being alive. And your hunger keeps leading you to the big questions, the deep questions of life, questions of meaning and purpose and God. You aren't satisfied with easy or shallow answers—you are drawn deeper. You are hungry for an experience of what is true, beautiful, good . . . what is meaningful . . . what is ultimate.

If that describes you in any way, this book is for you. Keren doesn't argue with you or require you to agree with her on every detail: she writes as a humble, gentle seeker herself, pointing you toward what she has found as a fellow seeker.

Second, you may be suffering from physical or emotional pain. As you'll learn in the coming pages, Keren is also on a journey of suffering. Emotional heartbreak and chronic physical illness have shaped her. She knows discouragement. She knows the pain of disappointed dreams. This isn't a book about someone who was in pain and is now fine and carefree. Stories like that can encourage some people, but they can leave many readers wondering, "Why were her problems solved and not mine?" Keren's journey in pain becomes her portal into deeper understandings of life. If you are coping with suffering, you will find in this book a trustworthy companion.

Third, you may be interested in something called contemplative spirituality. Keren discovered the writings of key figures in this rich tradition, and she has let those writings become her companions and those authors her guides. She has found special help in the extraordinary writings of a brilliant and fascinating woman from the 1300s known as Julian of Norwich. Keren reflects deeply on one image shared by Julian, and that one image becomes a window into the wide world of contemplative spirituality. If this approach to spirituality interests you, this book will be a true gift.

Like Keren, I was drawn to contemplative spirituality even before I knew there was such a thing. Eventually, someone gave me a book, and as with Keren, that book became a portal into a new way of being alive, a new way of connecting with God, a new way of processing suffering. Of course, when I say "new way," it was new to me, but it was also very ancient. Through the years, contemplative spirituality has been the medicine, the treatment plan that I needed to survive and thrive.

If you are a spiritual seeker, if you are undergoing suffering, or if you are interested in contemplative living, may I prescribe *All That Is Made* for you? I believe it will do your heart good and lead you to fuller wellness, wilder love, and deeper joy.

—Brian D. McLaren, author, speaker, activist, and public theologian

ONE

Meeting Julian of Norwich

In early May 1373, an English woman in her early thirties began to die. Or at least, she thought she was dying. It seemed fairly unremarkable. Various plagues, wars, and religious intolerance continued to take far more than the usual share of the populace of Norwich, the city in Norfolk where this woman lived.

We see her as young, but by the standards of the time she was nearing middle age. She may have been a Benedictine nun, a noblewoman, or a widow of the merchant class, though I agree with those scholars who think the latter most likely. Today we call her Julian, Dame Julian, the Lady Julian, Mother Julian, or Julian of Norwich, but this was not necessarily her given name, which we do not know for sure. Julian was most likely the name she received later because her hermitage cell was attached to St. Julian's Church.

We know precious little about Julian, and this is how she would have it, taking great care in her writings to leave details of her life out of the text, wary of taking any attention away from the things of God that had been entrusted to her to share.

With Julian showing all the signs of leaving this world, the priest was sent for. He came with a young lad, or curate, who carried a crucifix, a carved representation of Jesus on the cross. In Catholicism, a priest must give a dying person the last rites, absolving them of their sins and readying them for heaven. Julian's mind and eyes were fixed on eternity already, so in her understanding she was looking upwards, but the priest felt compelled to instruct the young woman to focus on the wooden figure. He probably thought that the sight of her Savior would direct her thoughts to her salvation and be a comfort to her in her dying moments, since she clearly didn't have long left.

Julian thought so too, and did as she was counseled, fixing her gaze on the crucifix before her. She was surprised to find that at the very moment she thought she was passing from the world, God answered three long-held prayers of hers all at once. Much earlier in life she had asked for, and largely forgotten about, three things: to understand the Passion of Jesus, to suffer physically, and to have three wounds as a gift from God (those wounds being true contrition, compassion, and longing for God).

These might seem strange things to ask for. But medieval spirituality was very heavily focused on suffering. Penance, martyrdom, and affliction held much more focus than they do today. For those of us not brought up in the Catholic faith, it can be tough to understand that the Passion and crucifixion of Christ are considered far more central in that church than in other denominations, including most of Protestantism and Anabaptism, which tend to center on the resurrection.

Protestant faiths tend to have empty crosses, for example, remembering Jesus' victory over death. Catholics and Orthodox Christians favor crucifixes, with the figure of Jesus on the cross. Of course, it is both at once for all followers of Christ. We marvel at the suffering and sacrifice of our Lord and the resurrection life that he brings. But in Julian's time, so long before the Reformation in 1517 that split the church, believers were encouraged to consider Christ's sufferings as a portal to understanding God's love. So Julian longed to experience or witness something of Jesus' Passion in order to better comprehend his love.

God answered Julian's prayers. She was already suffering physically during her intense and sudden illness. Before the priest arrived, she had gradually become paralyzed and was then finding it painful to breathe.[1] But in an instant, while looking on the cross, God healed her totally, and then blessed her immediately and overnight with sixteen revelations, or "shewings," that she might understand something of the nature of divine love. These revelations involved both physical visions and inner seeings, as well as locutions and understandings given to Julian's heart and mind, and often directly to her spirit.

At times they were visceral, featuring the bloody Passion of the Christ throughout, at others, full of a gentle tenderness. Julian understood with an immediate compassion that the visions were given not just for her at this moment, but as a gift to all her fellow Christians (whom she and I shall call *evenchristen*).

Over the course of a day or so, Julian received a series of sixteen visions.[2] One of the very first things Julian saw was a small round thing, "the size of a hazelnut," or as at least one translation has it, "no bigger than a hazelnut."[3] This is the vision we shall concentrate on in this book. There are worlds of meaning to unpack in all of Julian's receivings from God, making her work analogous to the "hazelnut" which holds all of creation. Just as she is told it is "all that is made," so too each of Julian's revelations contain more than seems possible.

Such was the impact of these revelations on Julian that she decided to spend the rest of her life voluntarily shut away as an anchoress in a small room, or cell, where she meditated on the things she had been shown. It sounds very strange to modern ears, but becoming an anchoress (or anchorite for a man) was a surprisingly common vocation at this time. It involved taking a solemn vow to remain in one room or cell, usually attached to a church, and devoting one's time to prayer. It was a serious undertaking. One had to have permission from the bishop and be pronounced mentally and physically capable to endure such a trial.[4] The rite to establish a person as an anchoress or anchorite was almost funereal, tantamount to agreeing to be buried alive within one small space. Nevertheless, those called to this life were so numerous that there was a Rule of life for anchoresses,[5] similar to the set of rules given to religious orders, which kept them grounded in a disciplined use of their time, essential for staying stable in such a life.

In a way, this was a similar undertaking to the Desert Fathers and Mothers, early Christians who sought separation from the world in the desert. This was taking oneself away from a secular world to devote one's life entirely to God in prayer relationship. It may seem bizarre to us, but it is and was one way of becoming a living sacrifice (Romans 12:1). We might understand it as losing one's life to find it (Matthew

10:39), or the selling of everything to buy the pearl of great price (Matthew 13:46).

For Julian, voluntary seclusion was a way to devote herself to the contemplation of all God had shown her, and to record it in written form. It was sacred work, and she needed time to pray and to chew over the understandings that had been entrusted to her. She may also have needed to teach herself to read and write in order to communicate them to others. She felt that this vocation had to be done in a solitary place, but she was also aware, as all true contemplatives and mystics are, that while being not of the world, she must remain connected to it. "In the world but not of it," as we often paraphrase John 17:15–16. As a vowed anchoress, Julian was bound to the place as though buried there, becoming part of the city.

In this incarcerated life, Julian would have had three small openings to the world. One was to the church through which to receive the sacrament, or eucharist; one for her maids to bring food and take waste and laundry; and one was a larger window onto the street outside, where at certain times during the day she would make herself available to listen to others and give spiritual advice. She was also expected to intercede for the place and people around her. Julian lived in a troubled and violent age, but it was also a time when people still sought out and valued those with spiritual understanding.

It took Julian decades to fully tease out the meanings contained in her visions and write down her conclusions. She began with a short text, which was largely descriptive of the visions, then wrote a longer version, including all the things she had come to know by praying through what she had received and experienced. She is credited with being the first female author of a book written in the English language. Doubtless she would be astonished that after being read by a few religious (nuns and monks) over the centuries, it would be far later, and not until six hundred years after she finished her book, that this slim volume would become a text revered and loved by many thousands of people, becoming a spiritual classic.

I wish that I had encountered Julian earlier. I started out on the contemplative path without her guidance, aged around thirty. I had recently been traumatized by a deep heartbreak and was also struggling to adjust to all the changes a serious chronic illness had caused in my life. Those included a relapse so that I was permanently in pain, exhausted, and mostly housebound, as well as having to use a wheelchair when I did feel well enough to go out. In many ways I had hit rock bottom, and deeper into prayer was truly the only direction my life could take. I was a single layperson with no religious training, just a deep longing to return to God and his loving comfort, giving him my all after years of going my own way. I curled up in his heart, like a seed, and began to let go of my worldly thinking and attachments.

It was many years later that I heard of Julian, and only after a number of slow readings of her small book and of those who have studied it, do I dare begin bringing onto the page the delights and understandings Mother Julian (as she is often called) has gifted to me that helped me make sense of this journey.

Whether or not you have already encountered Julian's work, you may be reading this book to learn a little more about this beloved Christian mystic and her visions, but also be wondering what it means to be a contemplative who spends many hours in prayer. You may have heard (or not) of the hazelnut and wondered what it is about, or what a small nut and a woman who lived in the fourteenth century, and a mostly bedbound woman in the twenty-first, can possibly have to offer you and your faith journey.

I hope that whatever your reasons for reading, there is something in this small book that will bring you consolation and comfort. If my words do nothing but pique an interest in reading *Revelations of Divine Love* for yourself, I should be well pleased, since this book is partly intended as a companion reader to Julian's *Revelations*. But I hope also that my own experience and insights will be valuable to anyone interested in the contemplative life, anyone seeking to go deeper with God into the realms of prayer.

This book, then, is a braiding of three threads: the subject of Christian contemplation and mysticism; Mother Julian's life, work, and theology; and my own insights into those as a confined contemplative. I hope it contains a few helpful understandings, coming from the starting point of Julian's first and most famous revelation, that of a small round thing. Together, perhaps we might garner from it some seeds for further contemplation.

TWO

My Journey into Contemplative Prayer

I was also around thirty when God entered my prayer life in a new way, thankfully less dramatically than with Julian! I began to put down roots into a contemplative life, simply and at home on my own, embracing the stillness, quiet, and time that I had been given. The new depths of awareness I discovered in prayer startled me. Having been brought up with just vague ideas about prayer within the Church of England, and having also been a member of a Baptist church as a young woman, I was being shown and told things in ways I'd never known possible. I knew I was beginning to grasp a way of prayer never taught me before in my Protestant life.

Weighed down by chronic sickness, and after a dreadful heartbreak, I was drawn back into the heart of God. I was wooed into the silent, spacious courts of prayer by having such broken health that I was incapable of doing much else. God did not break my heart or make me ill; the world and I managed that all by ourselves. But I do believe that both these things, offered up to God, can and do bear fruit that might be useful to my *evenchristen* (Julian's term for her fellow Christians).

Shattered and sick, I did something I'd never really done in prayer before. I stayed quiet. Not just for a quick moment, hoping for a "word" or a guiding verse. Not just as a pause before or after my amen. But silence as an offering, an opening of my time and my attention. Being with God, not hurrying past, throwing anxious glances at him. Sitting.

At first it was hard. Thoughts, distractions, my inner monologue were suddenly much louder. Desperate for attention, my mind seemed like a toddler who'd realized there were other things I wanted to do besides tend to it. I let them be. I read about "butterfly mind," which is a term for the flitting to and fro of our thoughts as we try to connect with God in prayer. Sometimes it seems as though our minds are being unhelpful and rebellious as we try to stay still and quiet, but it is just that we are not used to it! I did try mindfulness and meditation, and other things that were supposed to rid me of this troublesome cloud of distractions.

If I were to recommend any technique, it would be the Jesus Prayer favored by the Eastern Orthodox Church, "Lord Jesus Christ, have mercy on me," and its variations, particularly said or thought while breathing, simply as a tool to draw one's focus back to God. This can often be helpful, but most of the time I found focusing on ridding myself of unwanted thoughts made them more prevalent. In any case, I was so exhausted by my illness that I didn't fight them. I just rested in God and found that if I settled down under those thoughts and gave the time to him, that they didn't really matter. As long as my attention was focused on God, I was still spending time with my dear Father. He would listen, take care of it, be with me. If it didn't put him off, then I wouldn't let it put me off either.

I was helped tremendously when I found some spiritual classics in my local library I had never come across before. I read Saint Teresa of Avila's *Way of Perfection* and *Interior Castle* and discovered a new way of looking at prayer. Teresa was a Carmelite nun from the sixteenth century who wrote about her prayer life, visions, and understandings. I was moved next by the simple grace of another Carmelite nun and saint, Thérèse of Lisieux and her obedient heart, as revealed in her autobiographical *Story of a Soul*, published shortly after her death in 1898. The vibrant visions of twelfth-century German abbess, polymath, and mystic Hildegard of Bingen comforted me too, as I realized how God might speak to us powerfully using our imaginations, inner sight, and obedient listening.

These worn editions from the public library were anchoring points for me, teaching me a new way of relating to God, of loving, of praying. It was unlike anything I'd known before in my Anglican, Baptist, or Evangelical years. And even though I could only read one or two paragraphs on a good day, because of the cognitive exhaustion caused by my chronic illness, myalgic encephalomyelitis (ME), I drank it all in like a woman who'd been traipsing through spiritual deserts for far too long.

After years of communing, there was sometimes a subtle shift into a need to listen, to see, to hear. This I would describe as listening prayer. This is because prayer sometimes became not only about being with God, but also receiving from God. Maybe attentive prayer would be a more accurate term. This is something we must be very discerning about, since we need to be wary of our eager and overactive imaginations. But after a long time spent in devotion to God, we learn to know his voice, his tone, the cadence of the particular way he communicates with us. The best way I can describe this is like getting to know a friend very dearly. We can sit in companionable silence without any sense of urgency to speak or listen. But when we do talk to one another, we know each other's character and voice so well that it feels right.

A vocation of writing was given to me. Words often came pouring out onto the pages of my journal. Sometimes in a heavy drip, like honey, taking its sweet time. At others, in torrents that I could barely keep up with (or read later in my prayer journals). Some were inner locutions, as though, like Julian, I heard things being said directly to my spirit. Some were understandings, ways of seeing things, being offered to my hungry mind and heart.

Sometimes I received no words, but instead, images. Rarely visions, which are indistinguishable from physical sight, more usually "seeings" that showed me something visual in my mind's eye and which then developed into stories, ideas, ways of construing the world, or a new lens on Scripture, which always remains true. Even when there was just delicious silence, running under me like a cool and constant river, I sensed the unmistakable presence of grace. All of this, the images and the ways of seeing and understanding, I would call *mysticism*. As I do so, I caution that this term is broadly used across spirituality, but that when I use it, I am, as with *contemplation*, referring to a Christ-centered type of prayer.

Christian mysticism as it is generally understood has a long history dating back to the Desert Fathers and Mothers in the third to fifth centuries. These were early Christians who left the cities, preferring to live in small, eremitic communities in the deserts of Egypt, Syria, and Palestine.[1] They lived ascetic lives, believing that to follow Christ meant giving up all desires and property, and devoted themselves to prayer.

Christian contemplation and mysticism are often conflated, but there is, I think, a subtle difference. Contemplation is the silent devotion and consideration of our faith in prayer, often inspired by Scripture or nature, the considering of things, much like Mary the mother of Christ is described as doing in one of my very favorite Bible verses: "But Mary treasured up all these things and pondered them in her heart" (Luke 2:19).

The Catholic Church defines contemplation as "the simple expression of the mystery of prayer. It is a gaze of faith fixed on Jesus, an attentiveness to the Word of God, a silent love. It achieves real union with the prayer of Christ to the extent that it makes us share in his mystery."[2] Our experience of the mystery itself is perhaps what we would call mysticism.

This pairing of love and its effects are reinforced if we add Teresa of Avila's definition of contemplative prayer as "a close sharing between friends. . . taking time frequently to be alone with him who we know loves us," and Franciscan friar and theologian Richard Rohr's definition of mysticism as "experiential knowledge of God."[3]

It can seem confusing, and even an expert on the mystics, Carl McColman, counsels that contemplation and mysticism are "deeply related, and indeed almost interchangeable."[4] I would describe it like this: that Christian contemplation is spending time in quiet prayer. It is our focus and devotion on Christ, in short, sitting at the feet of Christ and gazing upon him in love and adoration. Thinking on him. It is the Christian life and the one necessary thing. Christian mysticism is the spiritual experiences that come from that, if any. So contemplation is the foundation and living relationship with God, and mysticism the way of seeing, being, and receiving that comes from that. Contemplation is the soil, is the garden we tend and grow in cooperation with God. Mysticism is the sudden inexplicable bursting into bloom of a flower we don't recall planting, or an exotic butterfly flitting across our vision to land before us, an unbidden source of awe. Both are gift.

Christian mystics, then, are people who see the truths God gives them, and have numbered many saints and writers. There have been particularly rich seams of Christian contemplative or mystic writing at certain times and places in history, such as the movement of the beguine laywomen across medieval Europe (in which Julian is sometimes included). But certainly we would number among Christian mystics Hildegard of Bingen in the eleventh century, Teresa of Avila, along with her friend and contemporary Saint John of the Cross, in sixteenth-century Spain, as well as modern-day believers like Howard Thurman and Evelyn Underhill. Julian of Norwich is often included in this rich tradition.[5]

A few words of explanation about the contemplative way of prayer seem in order before we begin. As we continue, we shall find Mother Julian a great teacher of this practice. After receiving her revelations from God, she spent the rest of her life, some forty years or more, contemplating what she had been shown and given.

Contemplation is mostly about seeing and understanding everything as it really is, and not how we assume it is, with the help of the Holy Spirit. It is about giving ourselves the space and silence to really look at things and understand what they are telling us. When we do this with God about our inner life, we might call it the prayer of *examen*. When we do this with Scripture, our contemplative reading might be called *lectio divina* (or *divine reading*—the practice of sitting with and meditating on a Bible passage and paying attention to how it is speaking truth to us). We might practice contemplation by concentrating our attention on an object (say a flower or a hazelnut), a thought or question we want to bring before God, or something else (an issue, a longing, a persistent emotion), within a quiet time of prayer, given to God. These things may then open up to us like a flower, showing us truths we had not begun to imagine in our mere mind's eye or logical understanding. Connections begin to form, our spiritual understanding is awakened, and we learn how to look at things with an eternal perspective, a heavenly gaze.

There is knowledge to be gained, poetry to be written, naturally, from simply sitting with things and fostering an open mind and heart, but many in the world do these things outside of prayer. Christian contemplative prayer is not the same as anything passing itself off as meditation without recourse to the center of all things, which is ever and always Christ.

Christian contemplation is begun in prayer, and it keeps Christ at the center. That is the only goal. To gaze on him. Whatever we might receive is simply a consequence of that focus. It is not about getting anything, waiting for anything, expecting anything. No one should embark on a deep or contemplative prayer life expecting only to receive. It is about love. Furthermore, those who enter a contemplative life who do not feel they have had spiritual "experiences" or "ecstasies," or feel that God has remained—through all their dedicated prayer times—quiet, still, even silent, have lived valid and wonderful spiritual lives. To each is given what is right according to God's will. The sixteenth-century saint and mystic Teresa of Avila posited that she might be of weaker faith than those who were not given spiritual experiences, since perhaps it was deemed that she needed them, and their faith was so strong and grounded that they did not.[6]

There is never any counting or comparison in the kingdom of heaven. Each of us is special to God, and each of us is different. No one is more special than another. In any case, all that is given is done for the benefit of all believers. Julian understood this truth better than most, humbly keeping herself out of the way of God's words and gifts, crafting the text of her book skillfully to create a deceptive simplicity resulting in clear communication.

Likewise, we must remember that everyone relates to God differently, some through music or while walking, but always from the heart and spirit to Spirit (John 4:24). There needs to be an interior stillness, attention, and focus, what some call centering, if that intimacy is to become contemplative or grow deeper.

Even after more than twenty years of practicing contemplative prayer I still consider myself a beginner, but the things I have learned I share in hopes of helping us all to a deeper, enriching prayer life, full of God's comfort and grace. It is good to first pray that what comes to our understanding is from God alone, and remain discerning. Everything holy that then comes to our understanding in these kinds of prayer, comes, most often after many years of practice, by the power of the Holy Spirit and through the grace of our Lord, Jesus Christ, after the will of the Father. It is a triune operation. And much, if not all, of what comes, when we have learned to sit and know the still,

MY JOURNEY INTO CONTEMPLATIVE PRAYER · 33

small voice of God, and discern his ways of showing us things, is gift. If we are given visions, seeings, and understandings, we might then call this mysticism. Julian called these things "shewings." But it all means nothing if not grounded first in prayer, and held fast to the cross. If all that is birthed is a companionable silence, that too is no less beautiful or great a gift.

Anything we hear, see, or receive in our understanding as we pay attention to God that goes against Scripture may of course be discarded. It can be a painfully slow road to walk, at first, with a great deal determined to steal our focus. But the only striving we need do is simply the work to carve out time to sit at Christ's dear feet. I cannot speak for others, but fountains of good things came to me from the Father's heart when I made time to sit in silence, longed and prayed for relationship with him in a deeper way, and spent so long with him that I began to recognize his voice.

I had no expectation or desire to receive anything besides love. Nor should anyone embarking on this way of praying. Our main motivation in prayer is always to give love. I did not know anything about spiritual seeing, besides having previously had one or two "words" and "pictures" either given for me or given to me to share. I was never taught that something that can be sensed as like a deep ocean of light[7] waited eagerly to speak to me of God's ways, wonders, and stories; that this was one of the joys available, if I kept giving myself over to prayer, falling into his will more and more every time. About eight years into this prayer journey, God sent me a Rowan tree, a loving man who is now my husband. He recognized what was blossoming and encouraged me, despite his own spiritual journey being quite different. On our first wedding anniversary, Rowan gave me a book, *Revelations of Divine Love*, by the very

English fourteenth-century Christian anchoress and mystic Julian of Norwich.

Everything about Julian and her beautiful writing resonated with my soul. There are so many deep things in what she called her "shewings" that can provide food for decades of prayer and spiritual studies. She is a steadfast partner for those of us drawn into contemplative prayer and the kind of theology that takes its starting point always from relationship—the cross rather than the textbook.

If *Revelations of Divine Love* were as simple a book as it seems, I might say that I drank it in. But Julian's revelations are deeply complex and full of layers of meaning, so I sometimes feel that I am still only beginning to peel small pieces of understanding from them. At the same time, her explanations are wonderfully reassuring and speak of a loving, gracious God we can come to entirely without artifice or fear. You cannot read *Revelations* without being in awe of how much our Creator loves us.

This is one of the many reasons that Julian's book has become a friend to so many people seeking to know God. Hidden for centuries, it is now recognized as a spiritual classic and has given us a whole new vocabulary for speaking about treasures received in prayer. As a Christian contemplative enclosed by chronic illness, I have been deeply blessed by Julian, and come back to her writing again and again.

For many years I have been chronically ill, and at the time of writing this keeps me mostly confined (possibly anchored) to my sickbed. But my "seeings" and "shewings" have been a great many, thanks be to God. After more than twenty years of contemplative prayer, I am only now in my fifties starting to collate them and herd them into books. Julian's experience was very different and extremely dramatic, but thanks to her I discovered that what was happening in my prayer life had precedent and wasn't anything to be scared or worried about. When I found the words *mysticism*, *shewings*, and *anchoress*, my spirit soared, and I felt awash with relief and affirmation.

Julian had vivid visions and impressions given to her over a very short and specific period of time and then spent the next at least twenty years unpacking them. Our experiences are very different in terms of timing, and of course I would never dream of equating myself or the small gifts I have received to Julian's deep, passionate faith and timeless sharings. But knowing that she wrote from mystical roots and was blessed to understand she must share them, even though she was "unlettered" (possibly literate or self-taught in English, but not knowing Latin or having had the same education as she might have had as a man) and cloistered from the world, has greatly encouraged me on my own path of believing deep, contemplative prayer to be a gifting and vocation even though, like Julian, I have no formal theological training.

THREE

Julian and the Small Round Thing

Contemplation takes your thoughts in many directions but always brings you back to Christ. What Julian does so beautifully is that, after she has contemplated her shewings for decades, she doesn't wax lyrical in her writings about them, but writes with totally clarity about what has been revealed to her in a way that can be experienced as nearly as possible by her readers.

She tells us what she saw, heard, and was given to understand, everything that seemed relevant or shaped her thought or tugged on her heart, followed by an explanation of what it meant. The book is divided into eighty-six short chapters covering all sixteen revelations.

Threads of clear connection web through Julian's *Revelations*. Everything leads into trinitarian revelations of God's personhood. Father, Son, and Holy Spirit dance as a family unit in threes through every image and thought. While you don't need to have read Julian to understand anything in this book, remembering that everything comes in threes will be helpful as we talk about her work. It is inherent to Julian's writing and thinking. It is almost as if the long years of contemplating our triune God filled her mind and heart with threes, leading her to see with trinitarian eyes. You will find this echoed throughout this book too, holding to wonderful groups of three threads, like Julian's conclusion that we are made, kept, and loved.

All that is written comes back to the vital conclusion that all shall be well, even when we cannot see or understand how. And when at the end of her deliberations Julian can sum up God's message to her and through her as simply love, it makes total sense because it is the motive she has ascribed to her beloved teacher, who is Christ, throughout her life and her texts. Love, always, was his meaning.

In her *Revelations*, which were written in Middle English (the modern versions we read are essentially translations, as English has evolved so much over the centuries) Julian sees "God in a pointe"[1]—meaning at one centralized point—which, though it sounds paradoxical, is a way of saying that she sees the totality of God in a way that helps her understand that there is nothing outside of him. As the editors of my Hodder and Stoughton edition of the *Revelations of Divine Love* remind us in a footnote to this strange image, "This mystical symbol is often used to express God's centrality, unity, immeasurability, etc."[2] God is the bright center of everything, or as the thirteenth-century bishop and theologian Bonaventure would say, "The circle with no centre and no circumference."³ Infinity can only be envisaged this way, perhaps, as a point running through everything at the same time.

This mystical, metaphysical—we might even call it quantum—way of understanding or "seeing" God (no one can see God in any real way, John 1:18) is about both holding God in our gaze with the eyes of our heart and understanding that this too is impossible. This visual and conceptual knowing is a powerful contrast with the seeing of all that God has made concentrated into a point. Creation being created and finite, we can envisage it as almost nothing next to God's infinity. What is important is to keep our focus on the brightness and centrality of God that is everywhere. That is the essence of prayer.

This is a difficult concept, and the reason I equate it with quantum physics is that it is seeing God as both concrete and abstract at the same time. The Christian faith, and indeed creation, are full of such paradoxes. Perhaps another facet of understanding God in a pointe is to think of how Christ is encapsulated in the host wafer, or how our DNA is encoded in every one of our cells. Light concentrated through a lens into a point may show us a new brightness, yet at the same time, the world around us does not dim.

Priest and poet George Herbert, born at the end of the sixteenth century, depicts prayer as "God's breath in man returning to his birth."⁴ This to-ing and fro-ing of love and life is a beautiful way to think of communing with our Maker and the contemplation of ourselves as his work. In a pleasing symmetry, the poem (another small thing) from which this line comes, entitled simply "Prayer," is made the center of another book, Dennis Lennon's wonderful *Turning the Diamond*. Lennon describes how finding this one short poem was like finding a blazing diamond that he wanted to turn to let each of its twenty-seven images, or facets, pivot and shine. He calls Herbert "a mystic with both feet on the ground."[5] That would be a good way to describe our dear Mother Julian too. Veteran Julian scholar Veronica Rolf says, "Julian is most decidedly not one of those medieval mystics who urges 'flight' from any and all involvement in earthly endeavors."[6] Julian can certainly keep us grounded both in the reality of daily life and the wonders of the sacred. She was not afraid to use herring scales, raindrops from the eaves, or even the act of digestion as imagery to help us understand the divine.

This image of "turning the diamond" is apposite as we begin contemplating Julian's words. We can gain a great deal just sitting with image after image. Julian herself was turning the diamond of her sixteen revelations for decades in her anchorage. We do this with scripture, of course. In *lectio divina*, we sit with the treasured words and ask the Holy Spirit to deepen our understanding. With a devoutly written book like Julian's *Revelations*, we can also gain much from spending time in its wisdom, careful to remember that it is an exploration of faith and given visions, rather than Holy Writ. Julian would be the first to caution us never to take her word over that of Scripture, or indeed of what she calls "holy church" or "mother church." We are never seeking new takes on our Christian traditions and beliefs, but a deeper grounding for them.

As we turn our diamond here, though it might also be a hazelnut, we must rely on the Light of the World himself to guide us. To begin to see the things of greatest spiritual value, we must start by gazing on Christ crucified. Then our seeing and understanding will deepen. Our gaze is returned. We are drawn in and then held in his hand.

The adoration of the host, also called eucharistic adoration, is a kind of worship usually practiced in Catholic or high church Anglican traditions. It's rare outside of the Roman Church, so much so that despite being immersed in the Church of England I had no idea it existed until I stumbled across it on retreat at a Carmelite priory. It involves simply sitting in church gazing in adoration at the sacrament, the blessed wafer of bread that will be used in forthcoming Mass or what we in other church traditions call the eucharist, or communion. Many will refer to this wafer as the host. I was skeptical at first as I'd never really understood the idea of transubstantiation, but adoring the host was a wonderful experience and I long to do it again. Since my health declined, I have to gaze with the help of webcams set up in churches.

This beautiful spiritual practice was still rather new in Julian's day. Feasts in the church are holy days commemorating saints, sacraments, or events, and the Feast of Corpus Christi (the body of Christ) was only established in 1264, then confirmed as official by the Council of Vienne in 1311.[7] But gazing on the crucified Christ, either in an imagination of the Passion or of a crucifix, was a commonplace devotion. Throughout Julian's visions and revelations, Christ crucified was before her sight the entire time, not only physically in the crucifix brought to her by the curate but in her spiritual line of sight too. In a counterpoint to when she struggled at first to bring her gaze down from heaven to the crucifix as the priest instructed her, there is a moment during the revelations when she determines not to take her eyes from Jesus to look up to heaven, rather choosing her Savior for her heaven.[8]

It is no accident that our language uses "held" when we speak about a mutual gaze. We *hold* one another's gaze. When it is a loving gaze, it holds us and all that we are. We too are contemplated. We lock gazes. We are locked into love, much as we are in marriage or parenthood. It's a loving, mirroring gaze. It's not something that's meant to be escaped from or broken (though in human relationships we sometimes have no choice). It's a way of being held or beheld.

Saint Clare of Assisi (1194–1253), another Christian mystic, and founder with Saint Francis of the now worldwide Franciscan movement, teaches us that focusing our gaze on the mirror that is Christ is the way to be transformed into Christlikeness by contemplation. In her third letter to Saint Agnes she writes:

> Place your mind before the mirror of eternity!
> Place your soul in the brilliance of glory!
> Place your heart in the figure of the divine substance!
> And transform your entire being into the image
> Of the Godhead itself through contemplation.[9]

Franciscan sister and theologian Ilia Delio explains Clare's meaning as, "Gazing upon the crucified Christ causes us to lose our balance and be caught up in the divine embrace of love."[10]

As we begin shortly to think on the vision of the little thing the size of a hazelnut, we can see that this too is also a picture of contemplation. If we want to examine something, we place it in the palm of our hand. We consider how it feels, what it weighs, what emotions it evokes. I've done this with objects and treasures in prayer many times to see what they might teach me, what scriptures and truth they might lead me to and what stories they might have to tell; to listen to the songs they are singing. A feather, a pin, an acorn cap, a coin, a dandelion seed, a cherry blossom can all lead us deeper into understanding God and his creation by spiritual extrapolations. This is how God tenderly holds us, and it shows us he is paying attention. He is hearing our cries, sharing our joys and laments.

Just as God gifted seeings and hearings to Julian and she was gazing in turn in contemplative love upon him, so God was seeing and hearing her at the same time, for in all our contemplations we are "oneing," as Julian calls the act of union with God, giving more and more of ourselves, our feeling and thinking over to him and into his will.

We would be wise also to remember that while we can savor the fruit of Julian's seeds of contemplation, and add our own into the mix, the origins of what we are reading and how they were received are of a different nature altogether. Julian's initial revelations came vividly and dramatically, over the course of a single, unforgettable night.

If you ask most people who have heard of Julian what they remember about her writings or visions, they will usually say one of two things. They will either quote the reassurance God spoke to her—"All shall be well, and all shall be well, and all manner of things shall be well"—or they will mention that she had a vision of a hazelnut. These seem to be the two things out of the whole set of deep revelations and contemplations that stick in the mainstream consciousness most.

Let us begin then by reading together how Julian describes the vision containing the small round thing, very near the beginning of the first revelation. The chapter begins with the all-pervading image of the crucifixion, leads on to Mary, then continues as follows:

> At the same time our Lord showed me a spiritual seeing of his warm and genuine love. I saw that he is all that is good

and comfortable for us: he is our clothing that lovingly wraps us, clasps and encloses us out of tender love, so that he never leaves us; being everything we understand is good.

In this seeing he showed me a little thing, the size of a hazelnut, in the palm of my hand, and it was as round as a ball. I looked at it with my mind's eye and thought, what can this be? And the answer came: it is all that is made. I marvelled at how it could survive, for I thought it might suddenly have crumbled into nothing because it was so little. And I was answered in my understanding: It lasts and always will because God loves it. And so everything has its being by the love of God.

In this little thing I saw three properties. The first is that God made it, the second is that God loves it and the third, that God keeps it. But what the Maker, the Keeper and the Lover truly mean to me I cannot yet tell; for until I am totally united to him, I will never have total rest or true bliss. That is to say, I can't have either until I am so connected to God that there is nothing between us.

We need to understand how small creation is and to perceive everything that is made as nothing, before we can love and have God who is unmade. This is why we do not have ease in heart and soul; because we seek rest in such small things where there is no peace, and don't know our God who is all-mighty, all-wise, all-good. For he is true rest. God wants to be known, and it pleases him when we rest in him, for nothing less can be enough for us. And this is why no soul finds rest until it can see that along with all created things it is nothing. When it freely sees itself as nought, out of love, in order to have God who is all, then the soul can receive spiritual rest.

Also our Lord God showed me that it is greatly pleasing to him when a helpless soul comes to him simply and plainly and openly. For the natural yearning of the soul, touched by the Holy Spirit (as I understand in this showing) is to say: God, in your goodness, give me yourself, for you are enough for me, and I can ask for nothing less to fully worship you; and if I ask for anything less, I will always be lacking, for only in you do I have everything I need.

And these words are completely lovely to the soul, and encompass the will of God and his goodness. For his goodness understands all his creatures and his blessed works, and constantly flows out to them. For he is eternity and has made us for himself, restored us by his blessed Passion and keeps us in his blessed love; and all this is out of his goodness.[11]

One of the first things we may notice, is that the "small round thing" isn't necessarily a hazelnut at all. Julian uses that everyday image to let us know the size of the object. Hazel trees have been around in the United Kingdom since 7000 BCE,[12] so a hazelnut was a familiar sight that all her readers could relate to. At the time, a hazelnut was also a commonly understood domestic measurement, an amount called for in recipes.[13] It's particularly interesting then that the word Julian uses for size is "quantitie." She might just as well have said acorn, or blackcurrant, or any number of other things. At another time in history, Julian might have said the size of a marble, or a ball bearing. But there is something deeply natural and universal about the image of a hazelnut, because we don't just conjure up its size but its shape and color too. And given how she goes on to tell us how fragile it appears, it is more than likely that she means not the whole thing, but the pale nut inside; the edible, crumbly part of the nut. At any rate, it was a great comparison, because once mentioned, this is what we see too.

Perhaps there were other things about the small round thing, like its color or texture, that made Julian think of a hazelnut. But now it is so ingrained, there's not much point trying to undo our own seeing. A hazelnut it is now and always will be! But Julian wanted us to understand that it was small, and round, and did not seem like anything special, just something that might easily disintegrate and blow away. So, what did the small round thing teach Julian? And what might it then teach us?

Let us take the three main characteristics of creation that Julian understood from this seeing: smallness, fragility, and roundness, and see what we may glean as we contemplate them. Fragility is placed at the center of this written nut, being the part that connects most with Julian's vision of Christ on the cross, and therefore this next section of the book may crumble into three further pieces.

GOD'S CREATION IS...

FOUR

Small

It is very tempting to think of the small round thing and immediately begin to extrapolate from it, panning out as noted Julian scholar Rolf describes it, as though we can leap into the universe from this one tiny thing: "It is as if Julian's inner eye became a floating telescope, zooming out to view infinite space, revealing the minuteness of planet Earth in the immensity of the cosmos."[1]

We can be eager to instantly make this leap and consider the Earth as "the small blue dot," as astronomist Carl Sagan called it on seeing *Voyager*'s famous photo of our planet.[2] But before we think of the hazelnut as a microcosm, perhaps we can just look at it for a while as what it is. A small round, brown, ordinary thing, something seen every day by those in Julian's time. If the hazelnut is "all that was made," maybe God is firstly telling us that even something this tiny and insignificant is an important part of creation. Maybe he made, loves, and keeps it too, just the same way he does us.

Perhaps the first thing we should be in awe of is that God's imagination, attention, care, and sustenance, his very love, can also be focused on something we would forget in a moment. As Rolf goes on to say, whether looked on as a metaphysical truth or in its own smallness, the hazelnut is asking Julian, "How is there anything at all?"[3] It is asking her the ultimate question, the meaning of life, the universe, and everything. The vision calls to my mind how Jesus tells us that the Father sees every sparrow swoop in Matthew 10:29. Nothing is beneath his notice. Whatever else we might draw out from the hazelnut and its significance, firstly it is telling us that this too is loved.

Clearly, the first thing Julian notices about the object in her vision is that it is extremely small. She uses the word "little" and says that it is so small she expects it "to fall into nothing." Since this tiny thing is everything that is made, it is tempting to imagine that it is full and compact, everything that is, squeezed into one minuscule space, and yet Julian gives the impression that it is somehow not dense at all, but vulnerable and fragile.

As a person housebound by chronic illness, I know how it feels to be compacted, squeezed into a small space. In these later stages I am mostly living in one room and spend probably 99 percent of my time in bed, propped up or horizontal. And though my seclusion is not by choice, as Julian's was, I have come to accept that for the time being, this is my role in life. To be drawn down into prayer in such a way as to become utterly small, like the very seed of myself.

Julian chose to be an anchoress. I get the impression that once she'd received these powerful visions and understandings, she felt it was imperative to meditate on them, not only for herself, but for her fellow Christians, both those who would read then and those who were to come after. How blessed we are that she understood this to be so important. She asks us to spare no thought to the "poor wretch" who writes, but to focus on the message that has been given her to pass on. This understanding was imparted at the same time as the shewings, that each of us should receive the Revelation "as though Jesus himself had shown it you personally."[4]

Thus the whole of the long text is focused on clarity, on communicating to us carefully exactly what Julian saw, exactly what she understood by it, and how God helped her to gain that comprehension. It is written in a beautiful, mystical style, because there is no other way to write about such heavenly things, but it is also surprisingly accessible. Julian has gone to great pains to write in a way that can help us receive as she did, in as vivid a way as possible, what she saw, heard, and understood.

Julian has rarely been touted as a theologian until more recently, probably precisely because she seeks to be so clear. There is no obfuscation, or a desire to seem knowledgeable, special, or clever, simply a pressing desire to communicate the things of God. She is totally aware of how her words will be read. The whole book is deceptively simple. She must have used the twenty years she spent meditating on the shewings also working on how best to present them, how to condense the awe and wonder of exceptional spiritual experience into language that everyone might grasp. We might say that the whole endeavor was akin to bringing everything that was given into one small, slim volume.

Like the small round thing seen in the palm of Julian's hand, as an anchoress Julian is soon to become a concentrated version of herself. The visions she has been gifted are to form the basis of a life's contemplation and be contracted down into the essence of their meaning. She is tasked with communicating these truths to humanity, to those of the Christian faith in particular. The visions that Julian saw in just a few short hours were themselves a concentration—almost like seeing "God in a pointe"—and she spent the rest of her life pulling and stretching them out to extrapolate their meaning. She would gauge and process her own reactions and understandings, which she then carefully drew back into a concentrated form, one small book, that it might bless others on the same path of faith. Contraction and expansion form the basis of the whole business, just as breath or tide do our lives.

In this contemplative life we let the world fall away. We begin to die to the world, to our very selves, letting even our bodies become still and quiet. And then the real work begins as we look upon Christ crucified. Gazing at the crucifix is to become again the seed of oneself. We must become and accept our smallness, and see ourselves in comparison to Christ, to God who is everything, all goodness and eternity. This is true humility. It is not for the fainthearted. It is hard to accept that though preciously beloved, in and of ourselves we are so very almost nothing.

Just before the segment on the hazelnut, Julian rightly tells us that Mary "is superior to everything else that God has made," qualifying this with, "Only Jesus in his humanity is greater."[5] Yet even those who devote their whole faith lives to Jesus through Mary, such as Saint Louis-Marie de Montfort, calling her "the magnificence of the Most High,"[6] proclaim her as nothing in comparison with God. Writing in the early 1700s, de Montfort opens the main body of his text thus: "With the whole Church I admit that Mary, being but a mere creature, from the hands of the Most High, is, in comparison with His infinite Majesty, less than an atom; or rather, is just nothing, for He alone is 'He who is.'"[7]

Every one of us, even the very best, is nothing compared to God. It is imperative to see this before we can go any further into his heart. For we must understand that we are not even so much as the tiniest thing—"all that is made"—in his hand that might disintegrate at any moment: we are not even a large part of that. We are one of billions of humans who have lived on one planet, out of all those created in myriads of galaxies. We are negligible in every term of measurement.

But this is just the beginning of understanding. Soon we will see that we have meaning because of the hand in which we are held and to whom we belong. That we exist and live by the grace of God. That we are made, kept, and beloved. This is what matters and makes us matter. Outside of God and his love, there is nothing.

Contemplation enables us to become one with Christ by gazing upon him. For that to happen we must become humble, else we shall be unable to see. We decrease, or as I like to put it, we "smallen." We retreat from the world and its distractions. We open ourselves up to God in prayer. At the same time, we experience a contraction down to our essence. All the unnecessary parts of us fall away, bringing us back to a pinpoint of light, one spark.

Julian will not mind at all if I use the example of a very dear cat here, since she is often depicted with one as her companion, so I'm sure she loved them too. When I was nursing our cat Melody through the final stages of her cancer, she got smaller and smaller physically, and it was torturous, but I could also perceive that she became concentrated into one central point of love light. I could almost see it. Near the end, it was as though she was a small star, a spark of light sitting on my lap. I sensed that she was becoming her eternal self. That this was the form in which she would go home to God. The earthly falls away as we head to heaven.

Scientists have confirmed that as life is conceived in the womb, there is a spark. Of what, no one yet knows. But it is where we begin. I wonder too if it is also how we end, before traveling onwards. As we near death here, and death to self in contemplation, we draw inwards down to one small round thing. In one sense, we become single-celled creatures.

For an anchoress, that was what sitting in her one cell meant too. A turning away from everything unneeded, knowing that God was all that was required or, indeed, desired.

The spark of life and love with which we begin in the womb is then perhaps what we condense back to. It is our sacred heart if you like, maybe with all we have learned and our wounds somehow held within that: this is what goes home to God. Growing is breathing in, dying is breathing out. If the breath is what returns to God, the cross teaches us that always, even as Jesus hanging there models the husk of God without God, we come back to the hollow, to the tiny mustard seed, the eye of the needle through which we must nakedly pass. The hazelnut must crack open and leave the shell behind. There is nothing beyond this that we can take with us.

In a mirror image of this breathing, perhaps the universe expands then contracts, like birthing pains, since scripture teaches us that the whole earth is groaning in labor (Romans 8:22). Our self-emptying is a kind of self-birthing then too, leaving behind anything unnecessary and coming raw and whole, the kernel of ourselves, to our God. And while this seems a physical act, we run to God proclaiming the resurrection of the body. We know that our whole, true, heavenly, eternal selves will in some way be triune, body, soul, and spirit, our likeness in God reflected, just as it was knitted together in the womb, a cord of three strands that will hold its integrity:

> For you created my inmost being;
> > you knit me together in my mother's womb.
> I praise you because I am fearfully and wonderfully made;
> > your works are wonderful,
> > I know that full well.
> My frame was not hidden from you
> > when I was made in the secret place,
> > when I was woven together in the depths of the earth.
> Your eyes saw my unformed body;
> > all the days ordained for me were written in your book
> > before one of them came to be.
> > > (Psalm 139:13–16)

We spend our whole lives condensing back into that point of light, that seed, that potential, and rejecting the world, knowing real growth will come by falling back into the soil of God. If, like Mary, like Julian, we offer our smallness, and the knowing of it, which we call humility, to our Creator, then he can germinate the Christ in us so that we can begin to become the mustard tree giving succor to the world. Though life will remain full of trials, Julian and Scripture tell us that the second death will not be able to hurt us, but be a moment's work, a gateway, a change of expression from sadness to joy.

After he had baptized Jesus, his cousin John proclaimed that "he must increase, but I must decrease" (John 3:30 ESV). This is exactly the appropriate response to encountering Jesus, and a great summing up of the lesson the hazelnut wants to teach us. We see immediately in any meeting with Christ that we are not important except in that he loves us. Our egos need to crumble away, we need to see the truth that we are nothing outside of or without God. This is another way in which we "smallen," and it is about humility and perception. Please do not misunderstand me and think that you are worthless, or that your life or love means nothing. This is not what I or Julian are saying. In fact, quite the opposite! This is really about what we consider matters, what gives our lives, our existence, meaning and purpose. That is simply God's love. We are fearfully and wonderfully made of course, as Psalm 139 exclaims, and we are amazing, intricate beings knitted together by God. But we are only those things because of God, because of who made, loves, and keeps us.

Just as we talk about magnifying God when we cannot of course make him any greater or larger, so we understand that it is in how we are seeing the truth that we change. We gradually come to understand that we are nothing and he is everything. Our smallness, our weakness slowly dawns upon us, and in this way, it seems as though we are becoming less and God greater. But it is our assessment and our sight that are becoming clearer, more truthful. I find a useful prayer is simply, "Lord, I am nothing; be my everything."

It is also about *kenosis* (the Greek word used in Philippians 2:7 for Jesus lowering himself to become human), or self-emptying. We empty ourselves of everything prideful and selfish, everything worldly, in order that Christ might be welcomed in.

Room must be joyfully made so that he can become the center of our lives. This is really the heart of what Julian is being shown in the image of the hazelnut. That we see the reality of our size and importance in relation to God, our Creator. When this becomes real to us, we magnify God and our self-importance melts away. We decrease, in that sense, and our focus and view home in on the Lord until he takes up our entire vision, our entire heart. He must become our life and our all in all. If we are wise, that will be our only viable conclusion. Everything Julian sees in this seemingly small vision has its end there and is drawing us to that point. Then we can know for sure we are held and loved.

My own experience of this is that it happens many times during the living out of our faith. Like breath, we draw in and expand, contract and let go. But each time we become more concentrated, more focused on Christ until there is simply no room left. I found that there was a time a couple of years ago when the whole of my being had become so utterly small, and all my surroundings, everything in my life, had closed in around me in such a way that I felt barely able to move. My mobility was (and still is) so bad, but also my circumstances, financial, emotional, physical, were crushing me on every side, above and below. The wolves and the brambles were at the door, the latter literally.

I remember sitting on the edge of the bed, aware that there was no room to move, that I was completely baffled in both senses, and that I was drawn right down to the smallest point possible. I was nothing much more than a seed of faith in God's goodness. That belief was all I had left. It was not, I want to explain, that I wasn't still a person, a mind, a being with all my character and history, sense of humor, personality intact; all of that existed, but it was tucked into this tiny seed. I am not sure how else to explain it. All that I was cried out to God within and through that faith.

I prayed to God that if he wanted me to stay in those circumstances for the rest of my days, then I would not resist or object, but would obey his wishes in all things. I asked and hoped that he would change things for me, and indeed in some ways he has, but I knew at that moment that what mattered most was that God's will be done, even if it was painful or difficult for me. Even if there would never be any relief or release till death. And even that, which I felt I was offering, I knew I would not be able to do unless he gave me the strength and willpower to do it. Even the seed of faith I was offering up was first given to me.

This is, I think, at least one way of experiencing what Julian is describing in her vision of the hazelnut. That we are so small and helpless, powerless, potentially always about to dissolve into nothing, and that what really matters when we see and accept that, is what God looks like in comparison.

I knew at that moment of deep surrender that absolutely no sacrifice I could make, even if it were terrible constriction lasting the rest of my earthly life, was in the slightest way comparable with what Jesus bore on the cross for me. To look at my own humiliation (bringing down to nothing) from being a healthy, functioning human being to what I had become, compared to Jesus' humiliation—the humbling of himself willingly from being with God to being a spark in a womb, having to grow, be born, learn to walk and talk, live on this earth for over thirty years, and then die horribly—well, it truly is nothing, relatively speaking, even though it was incredibly hard for me. Our deepest darkness is unbearable to us, and yet we can still see that

Jesus suffered far more. When Julian speaks of us or our pains being as nothing, she means as Paul does when he describes his great troubles as "light and momentary" (2 Corinthians 4:17) in comparison, in context, next to Christ and to eternity.

The doxology describing Jesus in Philippians is of help with this idea, depicting his true sacrificial life and death:

> Who, being in very nature God,
>   did not consider equality with God something to be
>   used to his own advantage;
> rather, he made himself nothing
>   by taking the very nature of a servant,
>   being made in human likeness.
> And being found in appearance as a man,
>   he humbled himself
>   by becoming obedient to death—
>   even death on a cross!
>
>   (Philippians 2:6–8)

FIVE

Fragile

DELICATE

Along with being small, Julian senses that the hazelnut-sized thing she is holding can perish. It is mortal, breakable, fragile. So much so that she not only believes it might fall apart but is astonished that it doesn't. She is being shown that the only reason we don't crumble is because God is holding us and holding us dear. Our very integrity depends on the will of God and his goodness. Scripture tells us,

> The Son is the image of the invisible God, the firstborn over all creation. For in him all things were created: things in heaven and on earth, visible and invisible, whether thrones or powers or rulers or authorities; all things have been created through him and for him. He is before all things, and in him all things hold together. (Colossians 1:15–17)

Our cohesion is in Christ. This makes me think of Saint Clare of Montefalco, an Italian Augustinian abbess from the thirteenth century who received intense visions of carrying Jesus' cross. An unofficial autopsy by the sisters of her order upon her death revealed that within her heart tissue, the shape of a crucifix had formed.[1]

Sometimes the truths we live out are deeply embedded in us. Such things will never "prove" the existence of God. Nor is tying our amazing God to solely demonstrable fact very helpful for an understanding of our faith. We can form worldly explanations around all the wonders of the universe, just as Clare's flesh chose to form around the shape of the cross. But if we deny that those same wonders are evidence not only of the Trinity's existence, but of their love, creativity, and beauty, then there is not much hope of us grasping the heart-knowing of faith. Yet even when we deny Christ's lordship over all things, the very stones shall sing it out.

Fragility and mortality are hard things to accept. We want to believe that we are immortal and invincible. Indeed, there is a part of us, aware of ourselves not just as bodies, but as souls and spirit as Paul describes in 1 Thessalonians 5:23, that is certain and correct that we are meant to be immortal and invincible. Julian is reassured later in her revelations that the souls of believers are kept safe and uncorrupted close to God's heart: "our essential nature, which he always keeps whole and safe with him."[2] So, in a way, we are following our faithful instincts when we feel this truth. But if our bodies were immortal now, while we are capable of sinning, that would be a very bad thing. I believe this is why, once we had become moral beings, God could not allow us to eat from the tree of eternal life while we were yet infants in the garden of Eden. "And the LORD God said, 'The man has now become like one of us, knowing good and evil. He must not be allowed to reach out his hand and take also from the tree of life and eat, and live forever'" (Genesis 3:22).

Eternal life in these bodies would have been a death sentence to us because we still had and have a lot of growing and changing to do before we can be made fit for heaven! We need to welcome the fact that we might fall apart at any moment. To understand that our view of the world and our stability within it can just disintegrate, because all of this is temporary. In his first letter, Peter uses Isaiah to tell us that this is part of the gospel:

"All flesh is like grass
    and all its glory like the flower of grass.
The grass withers,
    and the flower falls,
but the word of the Lord remains forever."

And this word is the good news that was preached to you.
(1 Peter 1:24–25 ESV)

We are, in this life, creatures undergoing transformation. We are changing from glory to glory as we gaze on Christ, going from caterpillar to cocoon to butterfly. I am not speaking of reincarnation, but incarnation. As in the metaphor of the silkworm used by Teresa of Avila, our souls are metamorphosing.[3] This is the work of conversion, which takes a lifetime.

Coming face-to-face with our mortality is crucial in that process of being born again. We must face many deaths before we can be brought to true resurrection, and we must understand what death is before we can see that it might also be simply a doorway into new life.

During my illness, a great many times I have been so weak that I honestly thought I must be about to die. Some are etched deeply into my memory. I felt that the very marrow in my bones was disappearing, that all of me was stretched beyond any limit of being able to bear the exhaustion or cope with the pain. At such times of physical undoing and at those when we feel mentally or emotionally that we simply cannot continue, we know that we are completely powerless to change anything.

This impotence can be something we sense in our lives or in the state of the world as well as in our hearts, minds, and bodies. We are living through a tumultuous time right now in the early twenty-first century. Postmodernism seeks to erase boundaries and meaning at one end of the political spectrum and embolden defiant certitude at the other (and confusingly, sometimes the other way around). We are witnessing wars, wildfires, earthquakes, climate change, a pandemic, the reframing of our economic systems, the rise of artificial intelligence, and the worst misogyny, prejudice, and political division I've ever seen.

Though such global awareness wasn't possible then, Julian's time and localized experience was far more desperate. The population of her home city, where she lived her entire life, was more than decimated at least three times by the Black Plague. She certainly lost family, friends, loved ones, possibly a husband and children. War was raging in Europe and bleeding the peasants and merchant classes dry in tax and fighting men. Religious disagreements and uprisings saw heretics being burned at the stake very near to Julian's church. The world was in upheaval, and mortality was evident to the point that you could smell it in the street and on the wind.

Julian was painfully aware of how fleeting life is, how we are like the grasses who are "here today and tomorrow are thrown into the fire" (Matthew 6:30). She counsels us to think on eternal matters, "for this life is so short anyway."[4]

In those times when I felt that the end must be near, I lay still (I could do nothing else) and offered myself up to God. I actually longed for him to take me home to himself, because what could be better? To have heaven and an ending to my suffering was not something I feared but was rather perhaps something "devoutly to be wished," as Shakespeare's Danish prince would have it. But there was always something sticking in my craw at such times, holding me to this world. Like Paul, I felt that whether I lived or died, it was to serve Christ, but the small round thing that seemed to grate at the prospect of my imagined floating off into glorious eternity was love. Love itself, love for my husband with whom I wanted to stay, and for those I might perhaps reach with the words I was writing. The thought that I might have more to do, even though I could not see how it might be done.

During both the most recent times I have felt this way, I was eventually able to move again, and I got up to go to the bathroom only to find it had been snowing outside. More small round things, each one unique and beautiful, just like us, falling to earth from heaven. It felt like an encouragement to keep on, especially when the same thing happened twice!

When I am at my worst, I wonder how I do not simply crumble away. At these times, I very much identify with that dear little hazelnut, feeling I might simply disintegrate at any moment. I don't know how I keep going. But I do know *who* keeps me going. No one is more surprised than I am that after over twenty-five years of illness, and most of that deteriorating, that I am still here and able to put words on pages. I look at how much God has shown and told me over all this time and am mystified. I bring him less than loaves and fishes and he weaves it all into feasting, with basketfuls of crumbs (more small round things!) left over. Serving Christ is far from easy, but it is full of astounding grace.

Paul and Julian both tell us that God can bring us back from any state of brokenness or defilement. "We are hard pressed on every side, but not crushed; perplexed, but not in despair; persecuted, but not abandoned; struck down, but not destroyed" (2 Corinthians 4:8–9).

God's expression of love, our being held precious, never changes. Optimism is always a feature of mysticism, not as a joyful feeling of constant happiness, but because we see in eternal terms, we understand as Julian does, that "all shall be well" however it looks now. It doesn't mean we don't suffer and break. We desire above all to offer this consolation that the more we see, the more we know of God's loving heart.

DISSOLVING

When I first read Julian's accounts, I was taken aback by how visceral they are. I had come from a tradition unused to dwelling on the horrors of the crucifixion. But in Julian's day this was all part of thinking on the Passion of Christ. People were more aware of physical suffering and death in medieval times, given it was all around them daily. In affluent, peaceful eras, especially in the West, these ideas have sometimes become sanitized or unfamiliar. We see brutality on the news far more now, sadly, than we have been used to for decades, but rarely close up. To clearly see the bloody sufferings of Christ as though they are happening right before her eyes is patently terrifying, but also, somehow, as Julian describes them with her lens of faith, a powerful reminder of Christ's love.

Julian sees globules of blood forming densely on Christ's head under the crown of thorns, that then run down his forehead and disappear at his brow. Like these, there is a temporal feeling to the small round thing. Julian feels it might shrivel up and disappear too. Rolf translates this as "it might suddenly have fallen into nought for its littleness."[5]

In her eighth revelation, Julian sees a vivid and torturous vision of the crucified Christ drying out and becoming utterly desiccated. The flesh hangs in shreds under the crown of thorns, so that at one point she is fearful that it will drop from his body. This pains Julian so much that she "would rather die than have it fall."[6] This is how she sees it while his body retains some moisture, but soon it becomes brown and dried up. As we read this horrific account of the Passion, we are struck by many things, one of which at this point is how fragile the flesh of Christ is, torn and limp. Julian's anxiety that it might fall away reminds us of her impression of the small round thing and how she feels it might simply disintegrate. Perhaps this is what the world or the universe or we look like when devoid of living water?

Likewise, as Christ's body gradually shrivels, it becomes more nut-like and the dark coloring of it strikes Julian particularly, seeing the flesh change color over time. The whole excruciating vision makes it seem to Julian's understanding as though Christ had been dying for seven days, even though it is just one of the shewings she receives over a few hours.[7] It seems in Julian's experience the same amount of time as we are given to understand it took the incarnation to happen, the world created through Christ, is how long it takes to redeem that same creation through the one who made it and holds it all together.

The fragility of Jesus Christ is emphasized. The vision of Christ on the cross is with Julian throughout the revelations, as she frequently reminds us, being seen both internally and with her natural vision by her concentration on the crucifix before her eyes. So there is a stark correspondence between the idea of creation being vulnerable and fragile, and its Creator humbling himself into that same state of frangibility.

Perhaps Julian is seeing all that is made at the point of crucifixion, utterly desiccated. Is this perhaps what love looks like when everything has tried and failed to defeat it, as though it might fall to bits? What is left of us when all the living water has been poured or squeezed out of us? Perhaps when that happens, when we have faded back into our smallness, our essence, we become a seed once more. Expanding the previous quote from Paul, we see more truth: "We are hard pressed on every side, but not crushed; perplexed, but not in despair; persecuted, but not abandoned; struck down, but not destroyed. We always carry around in our body the death of Jesus, so that the life of Jesus may also be revealed in our body" (2 Corinthians 4:8–10). Even as the sun goes dark, and God the Father has to pull back from his creation, it is all concentrated into "a pointe," and from there, gazed on by love, gazing back in love we begin again, we die and come back to life; life in Christ, who died with and for us that we might be redeemed.

Perhaps we too reach a point of singularity, and it could be one of the reasons that holy people (even if they are busy, or activists) tend to live simply, even ascetically. Becoming true reflections of God means we decrease and God increases, of course. And yet, those souls will shine brighter and larger than those who spend their lives accruing material wealth.

This hazelnut, this dried-up, tiny thing is what all creation would look like outside of its Creator; so fragile and unsustainable. If we could separate God from all that is made, this is how the latter would appear to us. It survives and is loved and cared for because God made it, keeps it, loves it, and he walks among its particles. He is the living water and the breath (Greek *pneuma*) that inhabits it so that with his presence, it becomes the beautiful universe we see around us.

This is not to fall into the mistaken view of pantheism, which professes God lives in all things, but to embrace something like pan*en*theism, meaning something of God is represented in all. We and all of creation and earth contain pieces of God, not that he lives in bits, but that each piece of creation reflects the Creator's glory and beauty. Humans, Scripture tells us, are made in his image (Genesis 1:27 and 9:6), *imago Dei*, so we are carriers of aspects of Christ, we mirror our Creator. Julian writes: "God, who is himself uncreated, has himself created man; giving his soul god-like qualities."[8]

In this way we are more than the desiccated, small round things we can become. Likewise, our faith begins as tiny. Mustard seed faith is all we need because it carries the image of a great tree inside it.

We carry the image of Christ and so in allowing ourselves to decrease, or condense, we can then become "little Christs," as Francis and Clare have been described, walking reflections of his light. Twentieth-century contemplative monk Thomas Merton saw this truth in his famous epiphany on Fourth and Walnut (another treasured nut!). He had been out walking and was suddenly struck by how luminescent everyone around him was: "There is no way of telling people that they are all walking around shining like the sun."[9]

Jesus shows Julian the small dried-up human he is without the living water and presence of God and that this is the dark from which springs all new life, because he created humanity as flesh, entered our world as incarnate. He humbled himself in this way because his love for us is so great and poured himself out completely, even to this grisly, dried-up death on the cross. Yet at the very worst, last, lost moment of this sacrifice, all changes— just as it will for us, Julian tells us, if we accept his gift of mercy.

Jesus shows us who we are without God, which is mere dust, "for dust you are and to dust you will return" (Genesis 3:19). As thirsty, dried-up souls, we see creation for the nothing that it is without him who loves it and sustains it, and we cry out to God. As Julian says, it is greatly pleasing to God "when a helpless soul comes to him simply and plainly and openly."[10] We might easily equate this with the famous sinner's prayer, or Jesus prayer, "Lord Jesus Christ, have mercy on me, a sinner," based on Luke 18:13. Jesus tells a parable about a Pharisee loudly thanking God for his own virtues, and the contrast of a tax collector's more humble attitude in prayer: "But the tax collector stood at a distance. He would not even look up to heaven, but beat his breast and said, 'God, have mercy on me, a sinner.'" The tax collector's humility and contrition are the truth of who we are, when coming before our God.

When we accept our littleness, we also understand our need for God and his mercy. We see our need to be loved and kept and we turn to our Maker to do this, who can make all things well again, and to the cross where this is worked out. We die, we are sent to the ground (of our being as well as dust returning to dust) and there we are reborn.

As our prayer for mercy is answered we become the Lord's and are re-fleshed, reborn, rehydrated by the grace of Christ's sacred heart giving out blood and water, by the receiving of this sacred cup of bread and wine, and we are sustained, saved, made whole in a way that can never be undone. As we accept Christ's mercy, so we become one with Christ's resurrected body, and as John 3:16 famously tells us, that faith means we will never perish.

It is like we are a piece of dust from which God longs to create a beautiful garden. He does not do this unless we allow him in, we see our own smallness, our own need for him, and even see how great an honor it is that he should love us and we love him in return in our small way, allowing him to plant and grow beautiful flowers. We are happy to be a part of the soil where our tiny mustard seed of faith allows the Lord to bring forth a tree large enough to welcome all kinds of songbirds and lovely creatures. In opening up our small, less-than-a-handful-of-dirt, no-bigger-than-a-hazelnut faith, we might find our Creator is able to make a garden fit for him to walk in, as he did long ago, in the mist of the morning and the cool of the evening, and we see that this is good.

I don't know if you have ever looked carefully at a hazelnut in its shell, but there is a distinct crown to the pattern, as on most nutshells. Stripes run down the curves of the brown sides. Not only does this remind us of the crown of thorns and the streams of blood running down from those wounds that Julian could physically see during her revelations, but also of the scourge wounds on Jesus' back. Again referencing Isaiah, Peter says, 'He himself bore our sins' in his body on the cross, so that we might die to sins and live for righteousness; 'by his wounds you have been healed' (1 Peter 2:24). Other translations call the wounds "stripes." Even Julian's imagery of the plentiful raindrops running down from the gutter is echoing here.

It is conceivable too that a connection is being made here on a spiritual and/or subconscious level as Julian thinks of hazelnuts for a comparison in size, for here is everything that was made, so fragile and tiny, looking as though it might shatter or disintegrate at any moment, and yet it is, or contains, all that is made. There seems to be no concern about that possibility in the way God looks at this small round thing he has made, only love. Likewise, Jesus, with the round nails extruding from his palms, is holding the whole of creation in those same hands as he hangs from the cross, seemingly about to dry up altogether, shatter into pieces or fall to bits. Yet out of both these images comes the immense hope that all is made, loved, and kept by God. We are given to understand that this is how he fashioned and planned everything, considering and coming into our smallness, our vulnerability, our wholeness that may fly apart at any moment.

We get the sense in both revelations that we are about to move into something positive, that God is about to work a wonder that will restore our hope and bolster our faith. With the small round thing, it is Julian's understanding that whatever it is we are looking at, whether globe or universe, creation or the human condition, it is safe and beloved. God is in control and knows exactly how it will continue to exist, because he loves it.

With the crucified Christ, devoid in Julian's seeing of all bodily water,[11] about to die in agony, there is a moment upon death as Julian sees it, where everything changes. This change first takes over his face, his expression. It is an emotional, relational thing. Just as God reassures Julian that all will be well with everything that is made, almost as if we see him smiling upon it, so as Julian was preparing and expecting to see

Jesus die, . . . "suddenly as I looked, the expression on his face changed. This change in his holy face made me change, too, and I was as glad and as joyful as could be."[12] Julian explains to us that this means that those of us who have died with him on the cross in a spiritual sense will cross from life to death, from earth to heaven in a moment, passing from one to the other without any painful process. Paul describes it like this:

> Listen, I tell you a mystery: We will not all sleep, but we will all be changed—in a flash, in the twinkling of an eye, at the last trumpet. For the trumpet will sound, the dead will be raised imperishable, and we will be changed. For the perishable must clothe itself with the imperishable, and the mortal with immortality. (1 Corinthians 15:51–53)

Similarly, Julian seems to move in her fears for the disintegration of the world and of Christ, to an instant, almost irrepressible joy in how much she loves God, and how much joy there is in Christ to have suffered to bring us salvation.

Everything that is made is held together in the bonds of Christ's sacrificial love. Our fragility and his are linked and both are borne out in suffering in this world before we are reborn into our heavenly joy. No matter how dead we seem, God can call us back into flowing abundant life in a beat of his son's sacred heart.

Perhaps the small round thing is a vision of what all creation looks like at that pivotal moment, in alignment with Jesus' suffering. Certainly, later in the revelations Julian insists that God's care is taken away from the world (as far as that is possible) as Jesus hangs on the cross: "As Christ was dying, even heaven and earth failed to function properly, so great was their grief. . . .

God who in his goodness orders the planets and elements to work . . . withdrew his order from both on that day."[13]

Perhaps this tiny dependent darkness is what we look like when concentrated down into "a pointe" after going through the black hole of pain, like a dried-out egg, useless and hopeless and yet somehow to God still loved and redeemable. Maybe you have been through such terrible times that you have seen yourself this way and wondered how on earth you might claw some way back into life and a sense of worth or purpose. Though this is how we see ourselves and our lives sometimes, God's perception is very different. He can always see the healing and redemption he might grant our deserts, suffering, and barren places.

This is particularly poignant for me as someone who very greatly (even desperately at times) wanted children. There have been long periods of painful time, when I felt I must be some kind of purposeless, infertile, dried-up, barren, and useless egg, unable to carry or grow life the way I felt I was created to. And yet, as a menopausal housebound woman I can look back lovingly at myself and see that it simply wasn't to be.

I may have looked at myself that way, seeing an unproductive, failed woman, but it was never how God saw me. He only ever gazed at me with love, knowing the way everything would look when all things worked together for my good and his glory. This wasn't to say that he didn't feel for me in my pain or perceived lack (especially as he blessed me with a wonderful stepson), but that he always looked at me with the same gaze of love. I was always whole to him. I can see that truth as I imagine myself curled up, dried up, seemingly about to disintegrate in the palm of his hand. He can suddenly with one change of expression draw me into germination, into a new time of growth.

This is true too of my physical illness and disability. He can see, all the time, the tree and its fruit seeding within me. He has given me visions, seeings, understandings, glimpses of heaven, in a very different way to Julian but just as real and wonderful to my heart. I have spent years pulling them all together and collating them into precious books, which I hope one day will bless and encourage both *evenchristen* and those who have yet to know God's deep and wonderful friendship. Because of this I feel a kind of redemption when I read Julian's *Revelations*. A kinship with someone who was hearing from God six hundred years ago.

Many modern commentators on Julian have assumed it is likely that she had been married and had children, and lost her family, since the plague had been so rife at various times in her life before she had her revelations, whether or not she had then become a nun. I think that given the times in which she lived and the wisdom she works into her book that this is indeed likely. Not many who had not suffered greatly could write with such depth. I balk a little when historians or academics profess this as certainty on the basis of the way she writes about maternal matters alone. I have never been a biological mother, but I too can think and feel with maternal instincts, and use maternal imagery, as indeed Jesus did, though a man.

We are not limited entirely to our own experience; we also learn by observing, through empathy, through love. We must be more careful not to make assumptions, perhaps. We can be sure that even if Julian did not lose a husband or a child, she certainly lost family members and would have seen her friends and relatives undergoing such great bereavements too.

Julian's questions, and the answers she receives, help confirm that we exist as Christians on that cusp between dying and knowing all shall be well (but not yet). We suffer with Christ because we know his expression is about to change to joy, but we must live in trust and anticipation of that, between those two realities, suffering edge dwellers, on the precipice of hope.

DEPENDENT

None of us is ever truly alone. Even when we are an anchoress, purposely shut away from the world, or a hermit set apart by God, there are connections to be made. We can still be friends with the moon and stars. Julian is often depicted with a feline companion, and it is likely that a cat was kept to keep down rodents as suggested in the *Ancrene Riwle* (the *Rule for Anchoresses*), but of course she would have loved to have such a friend. And she did see other people. She had maids who would come and bring food, empty bowls, take laundry and return it.

In addition, Julian had a window in one side of the cell through which she would dispense wisdom and spiritual direction to anyone who came. I imagine she would keep this to certain hours, since it is clear her main work in addition to prayer consisted of contemplation and writing. It was her window on the world. We know that she did this because of the writings of her contemporary, the well-traveled pilgrim Margery Kempe, who wrote the first autobiography in English, titled simply *The Book of Margery Kempe*. Margery is also known as a visionary or mystic but is of a very different quality to Julian, prone to being rather dramatic about her spiritual experiences, and constantly bursting into floods of spiritual tears. I wonder what the older, quieter, more contemplative Julian made of her. Another thing I have in common with Julian is that I write for my *evenchristen* rather than the world at large. To encourage us all in our faith and our suffering to show that God is love and love is his meaning in everything.

The ceremony that Julian went through to become an official anchoress is a lot like going through one's own funeral rites while alive. In a sense, Julian was consenting to being buried alive, entombed with Christ. In a similar way to those taking religious vows to "wed" Christ or become devoted to him, Julian was giving up her freedom, her time, her very life to honor her Lord. She knew she would never again walk through the streets of the city, or have a meal with friends, never again could she visit with family or gather fruit in an orchard. She was going to be cloistered, not with a community, but on her own. And this, by her own choice.

I find this extraordinary, as I'm sure most people do. I have been forced into a small space, a crushed life, where I can no longer do those things either. But I would love to! These are deep losses I identify with. Although I would never have chosen this secluded, limited life, I feel I understand a little, having lived like this, why Julian and others like her did.

In a sense, this was Julian's way of becoming dead to the world and alive to Christ (Romans 6:11). It may be that, having been through the whole process of bodily dying save for the very end, in a sense she felt she had died with Christ and was now a new creation. I mean this in the sense that having experienced that along with such a powerful taste and vision of heaven and of her Lord, that the idea of going back to normality didn't seem like a viable option. Perhaps she tried it for a while and just found her own understanding and perception of life and its meaning could not allow her to have an ordinary, noisy, busy life anymore.

Having spent a great deal of time in prayer, I must admit that there is a difficulty in processing normal life, and not only because my cognitive and auditory function is so quickly depleted by my illness. Those things are of course a huge factor, but so is the fact that, particularly after seeing glimpses of the heavenly life, of a new perspective, people are harder to bear. And this is meant in two paradoxical ways. I know that some people imagine that those who choose to lead eremitical lives, like hermits and anchoresses, are misanthropes, that we have a strong dislike for our fellow humans and just want them to leave us alone. That we don't want to interact. But if we have any understanding of the fruits of the contemplative life, we quickly see this is far from the case. People do become harder to bear, as I say, especially in numbers, not because they are unlikable or anything of that nature, but because human beings are so very glorious. We are so complicated and involved that to a person being honed into heavenly perspectives and sensitivities, it is exhausting to just be present with another soul.

Yes, of course, when you talk to God more than you do people, there is an element of being far more aware of humanity's foibles and inconsistencies and even wickedness (including, perhaps especially, our own). But hopefully we gain enough patience in prayer that this is not so much an issue. People can of course be very tiresome in other ways, whether we mean to be or not. Saint Thérèse of Lisieux recounts in her autobiography, *Story of a Soul*, that she was tested during prayer by a fellow nun in a way I can absolutely identify as I suffer from hyperacusis, or oversensitivity to sound:

> For a long time my place at meditation was near a Sister who fidgeted continually, either with her Rosary, or something else; possibly, as I am very quick of hearing, I alone heard her, but I cannot tell you how much it tried me. I should

have liked to turn round, and by looking at the offender, make her stop the noise; but in my heart I knew that I ought to bear it tranquilly, both for the love of God and to avoid giving pain. So I kept quiet, but the effort cost me so much that sometimes I was bathed in perspiration, and my meditation consisted merely in suffering with patience.[14]

Julian probably suffered with some of her visitors too. And yet, like Thérèse, showed enormous patience. Margery Kempe's gift of tears was not quiet, demure weeping, but the kind of wracked, loud sobbing that caused Margery's fellow pilgrims to avoid her at all costs. Some were known even to have changed ships to steer clear of what they saw as Margery's histrionics.[15] I confess, I doubtless would have been one of them, since I love quiet and loathe drama. But of course, Margery could not help that often when she thought on the Passion of Christ, she would fall into these loud and exhausting episodes. She came to Julian seeking reassurance that her gift was from the Lord. Julian gave it to her and gladly, listening patiently to Margery's woes over several days as she visited. Julian shows loving patience to her sister in Christ, and Margery reports that they had "holy conversation" for "many days."[16]

But the main difficulty in being around people for anyone who spends a great deal of time in prayer is that each of us is so wonderfully made. Just as Thomas Merton described so beautifully his epiphany that we already mentioned, we find that the light is so bright it is hard to be living life in the center of these sparkling, fascinating, amazing God-made fellows all the time.

An analogy for this might be found in the idea of visiting an art gallery. Many people could go to see a collection and look at all the paintings, no doubt drinking it all in deeply. Someone in awe of art and the skill of artists, or like me, who hasn't seen great works of art in the flesh for a very long time, would become overwhelmed and only able to look at one or two in a day. Human beings are (despite our sinful behavior) God's masterpieces. One at a time is stunning enough!

We do need to continue to interact with the world on some level for our mental and emotional health of course, and Julian's three windows connected her with the priest for the eucharist and confession, with her maids for everyday matters, and with those who came for spiritual guidance.

But most of Julian's time was devoted to prayer, to meditating on her visions and to writing her accounts of them. Clearly she still loved people; indeed it is that love that drives her work, wanting as she does to let the visions she has received bless her *evenchristen*. But certainly too, she must have felt that she could no longer be "in the world" and was certainly not "of it" either. She had entered a new level of being.

How long Julian had to wait after her visions before being able to become the anchoress at St. Julian's Church we do not know. The intervening time might have been agony to her, craving silence to think and pray, or it might just have slowly dawned on her that she had to give her all to these understandings, and that a way needed to be found. If, as was possible, she was running a business as a widow with her mother, she may have had some winding up to do first. If she was, as some believe, a Benedictine nun, she would have needed permission from her superiors.

Infuriatingly for historians, we just don't know the truth about any of these possibilities. But as people wanting to learn more about God, rather than more about Julian, we can take solace from the fact that we know this woman was utterly devoted to Christ. We can surmise that whatever position she held in life during her seeings, Julian eventually needed to go into hiding with her beloved. As with any would-be anchorite or anchoress, the local bishop, in this case the Bishop of Norwich, would have had to approve Julian's decision. She had to be examined and pronounced healthy enough in body and mind to undergo such a challenging new life. She would also have to show she was able to sustain herself financially with the help of bequests and donations as well as perhaps small tasks such as needlework. Some funds were needed for maids to cook, bring meals, do laundry, and so on. None of this would have been quick or taken lightly, which is just how it should be with any religious profession. But we get the sense that Julian had no doubts.

Revelations of Divine Love is a text by a woman completely dedicated to understanding and communicating what God had shown her. She simply needed to choose that one necessary thing and sit at Jesus' feet for the rest of her days. Nothing else could ever compare to the one she had already chosen for her heaven, and a way to devote herself, her time, her thoughts, and her words to him needed to be found. Running a business or in a religious community she would have been kept too busy. As an anchoress, she had to follow a simple rule, but her time was mainly her own to manage around prayer.

Just as I find it irritating when people assume Julian must have been a mother because of the maternal imagery she uses, so too it irks me when the fact that she uses quotidian examples of city workaday life is assumed to mean that she could not have been a religious sister. As though even enclosed nuns had not observed or could not continue to understand life in a bustling plague-ridden trading port. Anyone in these times saw water pouring from eaves, knew the ubiquitous hazelnut, and had smelled the herring in the marketplace. Many nuns would have been widows. What settles for me the idea that Julian was more likely of the merchant class and running her own household or business, is that not only is there a lack of any liturgical language or imagery in the text, but that during her visions she refers to "my" mother, "my" friends, "my" priest. A nun would have said "our," and more likely "sisters" than "friends."

Whoever Julian was before the visions, she was tremendously altered by them. I don't mean that she was a different person, but that her perception of life and its meaning must have been turned on its head. This happens to anyone who has a near-death experience, and there is always, judging by the number of books, interviews, and podcasts about these things in both Christian and more esoteric shops and websites, a great need to tell others what one has seen or experienced. Almost always, there is an optimism about what is to come after. Certainly, this is true of Julian too. But her response to the experience is about as far from giddy as you can get. She resolves to spend the rest of her earthly life bringing her remembrance and mind to the task of communicating these wonders for the benefit of her fellow Christians. Like Mary, whom she so obviously honors, she pauses and "ponders these things in her heart" (Luke 2:19). She has been given treasure and she means to refine it into words and clarity that will bless the world. Indeed, she comprehends during the vision that this is their purpose.[17]

Perhaps in some ways, Julian felt she had died to the world and been reborn in Christ. Maybe the anchorite ceremony, where she would have again received the last rites and been symbolically buried in/with Christ in her cell, taking vows to remain in that one place for the rest of her days, felt like a true representation of what had happened to her that strange May night. Certainly, there was no way to carry on with normal life just as it had been. Everything had changed.

I wonder if Julian felt, as I sometimes do, that she had been planted, rather than buried, like a seed, or a small round thing. A hazelnut in the palm of God. I rarely see anyone but my husband, who is my beloved, best friend, and caregiver. And even him, I can only see for a few minutes a day as I don't have the cognitive energy to listen and speak for long, making conversation difficult, short, and sweet. We too have had cats, as dear to us as people, if we are honest, and this has helped keep us sane in our loneliest times, and especially during the COVID-19 lockdowns.

I remember very fondly the times when I was well enough to go on retreat at Aylesford, a Carmelite priory in Kent. I had some blessed conversations with Sister Beth (Elizabeth Ruth Obbard), who has written some wonderful things about Julian. I heartily recommend her book *Through Julian's Windows*. We never spoke of Julian then, but at the time, Sister Beth was Aylesford's official "hermit," living a solitary life in a flat there. But since one of her duties was welcoming pilgrims for mealtimes and giving the grace, she met a lot of people! I found it amusing that the official hermit there saw more people in a week than I did over several years. Yet of course, like Julian, most of Sister Beth's time was spent alone in prayer. Not long after I last saw Sister Beth, she went back into contemplative life in a Carmelite convent.

"No man is an island," John Donne famously wrote, and it's true. We are all connected. Even shut away in a stone cell, our roots will dig down deep and meet with those of others. In her memoir *The Hiding Place*, Holocaust survivor Corrie ten

Boom recalled the solace she was given by an ant visiting her prison cell:

> And I was not alone much longer: into my solitary cell came a small, busy black ant. I had almost put my foot where he was one morning as I carried my bucket to the door when I realized the honor being done me. I crouched down and admired the marvelous design of legs and body. I apologized for my size and promised I would not so thoughtlessly stride about again.[18]

Even the tiniest of God's creatures can bring us connection, succor, and a reminder that we all belong. Julian could not have survived without her three windows (one on the world, one to the church, one for her maids), and there is a distinct possibility too that at nighttime she may have had access to the churchyard for exercise and fresh air.[19]

I too have windows, though I cannot bear much light, so the curtains stay mostly drawn. But perhaps my main window on the world might be the internet, through which I can share and connect with others through my art and writing. The relationships I have made there have often been deep, meaningful, and life-sustaining.

We are none of us self-sufficient. We are made for contact with creation and our fellow creatures, but it is not our first purpose. Julian understood, both at the time of her vision and over the long, mostly solitary times that made up the many years after, that God is our Maker and the one on whom we are dependent: "Only in you do I have everything I need."[20] And "He is true rest." But Julian's vision of the thing "the size of a hazelnut" goes further into that understanding than we might be able to take in. Unless, she says, we count all creation as nothing, we will not be able to grasp that God is our everything. We cannot rest in God until, of our own volition, our soul "sees itself as nothing, out of love, in order to have God who is all." I cannot help on reading these words but think on Jesus' telling the disciples, "If anyone comes to me and does not hate father and mother, wife and children, brothers and sisters—yes, even their own life—such a person cannot be my disciple" (Luke 14:26).

Both statements are about eternal perspective, about comparison, relative importance. The love we have for God should be so great that every other relationship we have seems like hate in comparison. It transcends every other feeling. Likewise, Julian gives us the sense that everything created is almost nothing, like this small round thing that's about to disintegrate: it is of no importance next to God, holding it, who is uncreated and everything, "all-mighty, all-wise, all-good."

The smallness, fragility, and dependence of creation Julian is shown in her vision leads her to understand that it is "nothing." It is an astounding viewpoint, and the point of the vision is to lead us into seeking God, finding the one necessary thing that we cannot truly live without.

SIX

Round

It is easy for us to think of the small round thing as being a depiction of our planet. The Earth was understood to be a globe at least as long ago as the time of Plato (around 400 BCE),[1] and it was certainly envisaged that way in medieval times, so Julian would have visualized it that way too.[2] With the privilege of having beautiful visuals taken from space, we now know that it is green and blue. The most important thing about it is to whom it belongs and why.

Environmentalists might see the fragility of the small round thing in the light of what we have done to the Earth, as it—or its capacity to uphold life—might seem fragile and about to collapse in on itself. Yet still God loves and keeps it. Another book of Revelation speaks of a new heaven and a new earth, and perhaps that too will begin from small seeds of faith. For many of us, the nut might be a reminder that we are literally all in this business of life and death together, and that we only have one home.

But as we said earlier, extrapolation is one thing, metaphor another. There are so many small round things in the Bible and in life: seeds of faith; the pearl of great price; wells; figs; eyes; coins. Each of them amazing and precious. From the husks of pig food to the ring on the prodigal son's finger, everything speaks of a journey from beginning to end, conception to birth, Alpha to Omega. Our very living and overcoming leads us through a crowning of thorns to a place in heaven where Jesus Christ may press a small round white stone into our palm, with a new, true name written upon it (Revelation 2:17). When gazing at the crown of thorns in her visions of the Passion, Julian speaks of the blood pellets that fall from Jesus' head. I think this is perhaps one of the most compelling images Julian uses, for this small round thing equals love, love that is suffering for us.

Round things are often full of potential, are pregnant with something, a hazelnut with a woodland, an egg with a flock, a seed with a harvest. Naturally this leads us back to thinking of Mary, mentioned by Julian just before she sees the hazelnut. She was the original monstrance for the host (another small round thing) growing the Christ child within her own body. It was her pregnant belly that held the pearl of great price. Such images speak to us of a small seed, enfolded in love layers, and growth of a light within a fragile shell.

So often we encounter Mary ensconced in stone and alabaster. It makes more sense to see her as flesh and blood. Perhaps we need to crack her shell open like an egg to let her come alive in our prayer lives and our hearts, just as we need to let our own solid, defensive masks fall away and let ourselves be human and real in our relationships with God, in our worship and praise. There are enough perfect statues in churches and cathedrals.

When I think of the hazelnut and of Mary, it leads my thoughts to the rosary. Each bead is a prayer, indeed the word *bead* originated from the verb "to bid, or bade," as in to ask. These are small round things we hold in our hands too, letting each one lift a request for prayer to Mother Mary. Julian would likely have used prayer beads or seen them used to count off praying the Psalms (Benedictine monks and nuns then as now were meant to recite all 150 psalms in a week).[3] The rosary as we know it today was not in widespread use until the sixteenth century, but Julian does mention the practice in chapter 69 of her *Revelations*.[4] I smile at the beads lying in my hands as small round things, knowing Julian may well have done the same.

A connection with Mary is explicit in the text. The beginning of this first vision is one of seeing Mary expecting her holy baby "as she was when she conceived," and it is impossible to read on and think of a small round thing in the setting of a loving hand without thinking of a fetus in a womb. It is a holy beginning for sure. The connection seems all the more vivid since the passage linking the two speaks of God swaddling us, wrapping us up in clothing to keep us safe. It is a parental image and brings to mind not only Jesus being wrapped up and put in a manger, but him being placed in Mary's womb, encased in kind flesh, to be taken care of. Mary is the host of the host and the incarnation of Jesus into the incarnation of his own creation begins here. Father God's love for all is drawn down into one small dot, and it will expand, be born, grow, live, die, and be resurrected to return to be as wide as heaven, holding all things together. Again, we see contraction, expansion, and back again. Out and return, always.

In her book *In Search of Julian of Norwich*, Sheila Upjohn has us think more deeply on the images Julian uses of Jesus as mother. Not in any sense of his being female, but that because he is one with God, who is beyond sex, he is capable of being both paternal and maternal to us, his dear children. Upjohn tells us, "Our efforts to perceive God will stretch our understanding to its limit. . . . So it is not surprising that we shall have to think in terms of female as well as male qualities."[5]

Continuing, Upjohn explains that Julian is saying Jesus dies on the cross almost as if in childbirth, quoting Julian: "He laboured until the full term, because he willed to suffer the sharpest pangs and deepest pains that ever were or ever shall be. And at the end he died."[6]

He dies giving birth to our salvation, our life. That he bleeds out for us unto death, he gives us life no matter what it costs him; this is a kind of motherhood. And we remain in him, as we are reborn, a circle of life-giving life.

In his letter to the Galatians, Paul also adopts this language of birthing his disciples even as he sees them also letting Christ develop in them: "My dear children, for whom I am again in the pains of childbirth until Christ is formed in you" (Galatians 4:19). Or as Julian puts it, "And our Savior is indeed our Mother for we are always carried in him and will never come out of him."[7]

In my own prayer life this has been shown to me as our home being the sacred heart of Jesus, which we had opened to us by the piercing of his side after death by the soldier's spear. This wound, that Thomas insisted on seeing with his own eyes and touching with his own hands in Jesus' resurrected body, is the entrance way into that womb where we might all be safely held.

In the tenth revelation, Jesus shows Julian a place through the wound into his side: "There he revealed a lovely and delightful place, spacious enough for everyone who is going to be saved to rest there in peace and love."[8]

Yes, the imagery is almost graphically female, as it is in Caravaggio's famous painting of the scene, where the doubting Thomas places his finger in Jesus' side wound. But we are trying to understand not only physical things, but spiritual ones, and the two will always overlap in this way. This is how God created our world. It needn't be balked at, but wondered at. Conception, birth, life, and death will all necessarily carry with their metaphysical elements, imagery of the female body, the womb especially, where we are conceived, knitted together, and made ready for birth. Jesus' human body was male, but that doesn't mean he cannot use female images and anatomy to explain spiritual realities to us, especially as the Father he is one with longs to mother us.

In what would be an agreement with Upjohn, theologian Eliza Stiles says in her essay on Julian and the eucharist, "While Julian embraces this female imagery of Christ, she never denies the historical particularity of Christ—continuing to refer to Christ exclusively with male pronouns even when referring to him as mother. Nor does she deny or ignore masculine imagery of God."[9]

In his answers to Job, God also speaks metaphorically of himself as both the mother and father of creation, using words like loins and womb. Human beings are embodied, sexed creatures. God is Spirit.

All this female imagery is very helpful in understanding Julian's theology. How can we not think of wombs and birthing when we are contemplating rebirth, seeds, and nuts? The same connections abound when we ponder Mary, or wounds in the flesh, piercings, and the letting of blood and water from Jesus' side, which opens up into the warm and beautiful Sacred Heart. Jesus Christ gives us permission in the incarnation to consider, rather than "abhor the Virgin's womb," as the Christmas carol tells us. We can think on female biology, on consent, conception, pregnancy, and crowning. All of this becomes holy, or rather, we also finally see that it is holy, as we pray. No wonder, presented with all this, that Julian has no hesitation in framing Christ as our mother.

This divine motherhood, explains Julian, like its earthly counterpart, also entails letting us fall and be disciplined. Even when our sins feel overwhelming, Julian tells us, we can run to God as a good parent, "But at such times our kindly Mother does not want us to run away, he would hate nothing more. No, he wants us to be like a little child, who rushes to its mother for help whenever it is hurt or scared."[10]

Julian tells us in the first revelation that the whole time the visions were playing out before her eyes she was also seeing Jesus on the cross.[11] She sees his blood under the crown of thorns forming thickly as pellets, then running down into brighter red circles onto his forehead like fish scales. There is no way this roundness is not connected to the small round thing. And the round thing is held in the palm of the hand, which is where, traditionally, the nails were thought to have passed through. We might be given to understand that this place where all creation is held so tenderly is also the site of one of the wounds of Christ. We sit in the center of Christ's woundedness and reflect the shape of his crucified blood. This is a beautiful, heartrending "oneing." It shows us also that everything that is made is done so through Christ, and through his sacrifice. We are one with his suffering, which in turn links back to our fragility.

It is in the palm of the hand that we roll and make balls of clay and dough too, a place of creation. When Jesus does this with the mud and his spit in John 9, using his hands when he heals the blind man's sight, part of me wonders if he is creating a new eye. He is certainly giving the man clarity of vision in other ways as well as physically. If we are practicing contemplative prayer, we are constantly brought back to Christ, and it is clear that Julian is, too, bringing to mind gospel truths and stories both clearly and implicitly with her descriptions.

Nor is it any wonder, when considering small round things, if we think of eyes and sight, since this vision is not only being seen by Julian with both inner and outer eyes, but because the whole thing is about perception. The lens through which we see everything is round. We perceive with eyes, binoculars, telescopes, microscopes. We view faraway galaxies and the microbes under our noses through the round window. It is not just our eyes that are round, but our seeing too.

Roundness is an image of wholeness as well as emptiness. A sphere is complete and is also the building block of the universe, egg, nut, seed, cell, planet, atom, photon. It is an image of perfection in that sense, needing nothing to be added or taken away. A perfect circle, we say, and the artists among us recall that it is the hardest thing to draw freehand. The halo around every iconic saint, and the total of God's promise in a rainbow, which seen from above is a circle. My husband Rowan reminded me that all pliant matter in zero gravity will become round, because of the equal pressure exerted upon it at every point. Many of us have seen the footage of astronauts squeezing juice out of a carton and seeing it clump into small spheres which can then be swallowed.

Roundness is a form we revert to, a remembering of the shape of our cells, or our time in the womb. When we are very scared, we curl up, become fetal. We clench our hands into fists when we feel threatened or scared. Moisture hitting surfaces becomes spherical. The tears we cry and the blood we shed comes in droplets, just like the ones Julian sees fall from Jesus' forehead.

A globe can perhaps be a symbol of the infinite, of the constant. The turning of orbits and things returning to their beginning. Perhaps we might see there the three dimensions of the Trinity and its perfect symmetry. The turning of heavenly bodies, passing through day and night, dark and light, and the seasons. Flowers and fruit, seeds and nuts, ova and shells, even bubbles and stitches, all have roundness at the heart of them, wrapping something around something smaller, as does the Madonna's belly holding the host. We even think of nothing as a round thing. All beginnings and endings seem to be round. Roundness holds everything and nothing. A zero is a circle holding nothing yet is the beginning of both mathematics and the Fibonacci sequence that we see everywhere in nature. Again we come back to Bonaventure's definition of God as "the circle with no centre and no circumference."[12]

God is the arms holding his omnipresent circumference around my emptiness. God is the ground of my praying (as he tells Julian) and in him I plant my seed of almost nothing, trusting him with its potential. Each of us is an anchor-hold. A small nothing enclosed in the love, *l'oeuf*, 0, arms of God, our nothing wrapped and swaddled in his everything.

As I am writing this section, God gives me a picture in prayer. I see a circle with a center point and the cross overlaying both. Perhaps the Celtic cross, but my first thought is that these are the enfolding loving bounds of God around our self, our nothing. In the center our mustard seed of faith, held in the palm of God. One drop of Christ's blood falls on to its small, desiccated roundness and ripples out like a stone dropping into a pond. Ripples of concentric love constantly wave out, and from these grow faith, growing the cross in our lives. Our smallness, conceived in the bounds of God, becomes consumed by love.

Through Julian's deeper vision, we are being shown how beloved something is despite its smallness, relating to our own, and that this is in relation to God's love and importance, so that we are not looking with a gaze that measures (since God is infinite and the only way we can even conceive of "seeing" him is in a pointe that includes everything) but that needs to understand. We gaze to conceive of the coexisting truths that we are both nothing, made, loved, and kept by the one who is everything, AND that we have meaning because we are made, loved, and kept by him. This is our inescapable and welcome conclusion once we have grasped our smallness, our powerlessness. These thoughts are spoken to Julian's spirit by God himself, as she wonders how "all that is made" does not fall to bits. We can be certain then, that we are made, kept, and loved because God is our "Maker, Keeper, and Lover."

GOD'S CHILDREN ARE...

SEVEN

Made

In describing the meaning of her vision, Julian tells us, "He has made us for himself."[1] We are part of creation. We have a Creator. We are not an accident, but beings made for a purpose. We are created out of love. Love made us. We see this truth mirrored around us, of course, in procreation, where children are conceived into a loving family (we hope). If by lovemaking in a marriage, this is a giving and receiving of physical love between two people within a covenant of love. Love cannot help but give itself out over and over. We see God's love poured out too in the creation of adopted and blended families, mirroring the fact that he has adopted us as his own beloved children (Ephesians 1:5). God has not created us that he might be loved but that he might love us. We are his beloved children. It is our purpose, it is why we exist, because God loved us into being, loves, makes, and keeps us still.

This is the good news of the gospel, that we are beloved, kept, and restored to the one who created us. It is fundamental to an understanding of that gospel to know that we are created beings. We have not appeared by chance. We have been fashioned, made, created.

In Julian's time this would not have been a controversial idea. Now of course, we have Darwin's theory of evolution to consider. While we can see that the universe abides by natural laws of cause and effect, of growth and reproduction, we cannot as Christians believe that everything has come into being by chance, nor that life continues or is sustained purely through chance events. This doesn't mean that we can't accept the existence of inbuilt mechanisms of adaption. But we believe that these things are God-ordained and that the one who used them and built them into the works can see how they will, do, and have worked.

In many ways, this is even more astonishing than the idea that Adam and Eve were created as if we took the creation story in Genesis literally. I quite often like to take biblical myths and stories both literally and figuratively at the same time. I am quite happy to believe these two people existed in some way as the mother and father of the human race and that this is also a deep and mystical account of God's relationship with the first human beings. That said, it is in some ways even more astonishing and not at all at odds with the deep truths of the story, if we came to be how we are by a process of evolution. The scientific evidence for this is, of course, compelling. When I had a brief period as an evangelical, it was one of the things that I simply could not dismiss, despite encouragement to do so. Science, to me, is about finding out how God maintains the universe. Fascinating, and always far more complicated than we can fathom with our limited imaginations and intelligence. Evolution is sheer brilliance.

In any case, whether we were placed in the garden of Eden, or came to be there over millions of years, or both, clearly some parts of creation have evolved and all of life appears to have been endowed with the capability to both adapt and reproduce. God gave us and all life the ability to improve, to become more comfortable and secure in our environments. That is something to be thankful for. We serve a God who is far-seeing and who, unlike us, understands chaos theory. It's simply one of the tools he uses. He knows exactly how everything will turn out, and loves every stage along the way. He loves the egg, caterpillar, cocoon, and winged creature that we are. We can trust him with our own development, and that of the cosmos in which we live.

However we came to be, we were made by God. We were intended. We are named and loved by him. We are his. Each one of us is knitted together in our mother's womb as triune reflections of our Maker; body, spirit, and soul, a strand of three cords not easily broken. We are fearfully and wonderfully made as individuals as well as being one of a species and part of a community. "So God created mankind in his own image, in the image of God he created them; male and female he created them" (Genesis 1:27). God made all and pronounced it good (Genesis 1:31).

Because we have a heavenly Father, we carry within us our true image, which is a facet of the image of Christ. As we've said, this is usually called the *imago Dei*, or image of God. When we say we are self-emptying, decreasing, or embracing *kenosis*, we mean we are casting off our old selves, cracking our shells open, letting our God-given image and wholeness come to light by gazing at the source of that life, who is Christ.

Beloved saints like Clare of Assisi tell us that this adoration also causes transformation, that we are built to become reflections of Christ. The beautiful description she gave to Saint Agnes of gazing at Christ as in a mirror (see page 42) also shows us what Julian herself did, both in the hours she looked upon the crucifix receiving her revelations, and during the many decades she spent contemplating all she saw.

Franciscan scholar and nun Ilia Delio describes Clare's understanding of this transformative contemplation thus: "The more we allow ourselves to be transformed by the Spirit of love, the more we become ourselves, and the more we become ourselves, the more we are like God. Each of us is created in a unique way to express the love of God in the world and to show the face of God to the world."[2]

In addition, we carry the seeds of all our descendants within our genes and DNA—and the echoes of our ancestors too. We hold the past and future within us. We are all hazelnuts with the potential to become woodlands. And this is true in other ways for everyone, including those of us not blessed with being parents. We can nurture future generations, be good aunts, uncles, cousins, friends, mentors to those younger, and we can also be makers. We are creative creatures, made in the image of a Creator. We can gift the world art, stories, inventions, and many things, such as laughter and wisdom, that we might not at first put in that category of making. But anything we leave behind us that will be life-enhancing for others is our way of adding to the joy of creation. Delio might call that the spiritual fragrance that we bequeath to the world. "Although the saints are seldom recognized as saints in their lifetimes, what makes them stand apart after their deaths is the fragrance of love they leave behind."[3] Perhaps we might even call this a kind of spiritual evolution. We are moving the human race nearer to wholeness, to joy, to love, to God.

We are created, then, with the seed of love in us, with the possibility of growth and adaption and re-creation. Because we see we are beloved, we see the possibility of loving God in return and that we might do his will. We see that everything was and is created by and for himself, who is love, and that our part in that is also to become love, to share love, to shine with love.

There is a dormancy about this small round thing, a sense that it might do something, even if that might be only to disintegrate, fall apart, open. It is made, kept, and loved. It is his, not ours. It is delicate. It is Schrödinger's nut, for we are not sure if it is alive or dead. To Julian it seems barely alive, as though it might shrivel and die.

But that it reminds her of a nut is telling. Given that it comes straight after God showing her his love as analogous to clothing, it might have made sense for her to see this small round thing as akin to a button or a bead. But it is clearly organic in her understanding. There is some kind of potential here. There is a folded, curled, fetal quality to it. Like an egg, a seed, a nut-like something. One feels in God's hands it might germinate or break into new life, hatch, even. Maybe sprout wings.

The germ of an idea might live here. A beginning. Like the Word to write this book, which came via my dear husband running up the stairs with an instruction about a book to do with Julian's hazelnut, just received in prayer. Seeds are of course an image Jesus uses in his teachings about the kingdom of heaven. There is no harvest later unless one kernel of wheat first falls to the ground (John 12:24). In the same way, he gives us to understand that we cannot enter the Resurrection Life in this one unless we allow everything else but our faith to crumble away. We must give or we shall never receive. Our lives must be sacrificed, broken open, let go, if we are to inherit the kingdom of God. In his first letter to the Corinthians, Paul spells this out as regards the resurrection of the body, shaking his head at the foolishness of those who worry about their earthly remains.

> But someone will ask, "How are the dead raised? With what kind of body will they come?" How foolish! What you sow does not come to life unless it dies. When you sow, you do not plant the body that will be, but just a seed, perhaps of wheat or of something else. . . . So will it be with the resurrection of the dead. The body that is sown is perishable, it is raised imperishable; it is sown in dishonor, it is raised in glory; it is sown in weakness, it is raised in power; it is sown a natural body, it is raised a spiritual body.
>
> If there is a natural body, there is also a spiritual body. (1 Corinthians 15:35–37, 42–44)

Everything that is made has to crack open to grow. Globes and firmaments within firmaments, a nut of universes that fit neatly inside one another like Russian dolls. We do not know the color of the small round thing, but since it reminds Julian of a nut it might well be brown, the color of seed and earth and humility. Certainly that its size makes her think of a nut is significant. We think of that kernel of wheat, and also the mustard seed that Jesus speaks of as a beginning, and later equates to the smallness of our faith not mattering.

> Again he said, "What shall we say the kingdom of God is like, or what parable shall we use to describe it? It is like a mustard seed, which is the smallest of all seeds on earth. Yet

when planted, it grows and becomes the largest of all garden plants, with such big branches that the birds can perch in its shade." (Mark 4:30–32)

What matters is that it is a beginning at all. We can only provide that beginning, that spark, that faith, that obedience, that yes, as Mary does, and God takes it and the processes of heaven take over. It is not so strange that his own creation follows those same laws of conception, growth, and birth, for even universes have to start somewhere, and who knows whether the seed of a cosmos in God's hand might not resemble a small round nut?

We belong utterly to God. We cannot grow or become anything more outside of his gaze, his holding, his love, and again I quote the precious truth told Julian, "He made us for himself." It is important that we understand God's motives for creation. In a way, it is impossible for us to do that because we always fall into the trap of ascribing human motives to God. The divine being is so far beyond our understanding that our attempts to work it out are generally meager and way off the mark. As with God's greatness, love, and character, we can only catch glimpses of how wonderful and truly good he is.

We might imagine in our smallness that God created us as beings to love. Company, people to relate to. But God already had the hordes of angels in heaven. We are not cosmically longed-for pets. God has no need of us. That's a hard truth to take in. God is complete in and of himself, the Trinity already contains a universe of love dancing between Father, Son, and Holy Spirit. It does not *need* further expression. But that love is so great that it spills out *into* more expression. Indeed, I don't believe it can help itself. Like a fountain constantly bubbling over, or a fire sending sparks up into the sky, the love at the heart of everything is exploding with yet more love, with joy, with beauty, with grace, with every good thing. Perhaps the very act of creation is like love bursting into song.

In truth, we can't ever know. But I think we probably come closest to understanding when we become, or see others become, parents. The embodied, enacted love between a woman and a man creates a new life, a spark, another being. It brings life into the world. If all goes well, it is a natural, joyous process, but of course there is pain and cost too. That love has engendered something new, and not just something, but someone. There is a powerful, sacred bond, and the family grows beyond two people. We see this everywhere in our world. Wherever life exists, there is an unstoppable urge to create more of it. Cells splitting in half, creatures swapping fluids, giving themselves to one another. And this too is a reflection of who God is, the God of loving abundance.

As a stepparent (a joy and privilege in itself) I appreciate that love brings families together and creates new ones. There is a deep joy present when we welcome small ones into our lives, even small animals! God did not create us to be playthings or to satisfy some longing, or because he needed anything from us, but because he couldn't help his love from blessing himself with yet more love. He loves us with such a deep and unfathomable love, that it is impossible for us to measure or understand it. Even our wildest guesses at the how and why and how much he loves us miss the truth by light-years. We cannot conceive of how dear we are to him. So much so that along with our lives, our whole eternity is planned and understood.

Jesus gave us a small inkling of this when he told us that God knows the number of hairs on our heads at any one time. I like to think he chose that particular example both because it is a very large number (for most of us!) and because it is constantly changing. We only need look at our hairbrushes to know that.

We are each carrying an aspect of God, a reflection of his character, of his being, our *imago Dei* as we said earlier when we looked at Genesis 1:27, and like him, we are partly Spirit, that we might both communicate with and return to our God someday. "The Spirit himself testifies with our spirit that we are God's children. Now if we are children, then we are heirs—heirs of God and co-heirs with Christ, if indeed we share in his sufferings in order that we may also share in his glory" (Romans 8:16–17). These two verses tell us, in a nutshell (even one so small as a hazelnut), the wonderful news of the gospel, that we are children of God, and that we can participate with Christ's sufferings and glory. Paul, as Julian, sees the meaning of our lives laid out with eternal vision.

No one, then, knows us as God does. Keeper of our DNA, knower of our cares, counter of every hair on our heads and their changing number by the tides of combs and age. No one else can claim us for their own. The enemy tries, but he is only the father of lies. The truth will see its progeny home. There is only one Creator, one Maker of heaven and earth.

The Lord God knitted us together in our mothers' wombs and knew us even before we began there: "Before I formed you in the womb I knew you, before you were born I set you apart; I appointed you as a prophet to the nations" (Jeremiah 1:5).

Some parents keep a baby journal, some of us a diary, and very few keep it up consistently. Life gets in the way somehow. Diligence is rare. Some of us journal but then can't read our own handwriting. God keeps everything. He records each moment in the book of life and saves every one of our tears in his bottles

(Psalm 56:8; Luke 10:20; Philippians 4:3; Revelation 20:12). When I try to imagine this, I think of the end scenes of *Raiders of the Lost Ark* or of God presiding carefully over racks of books, scrolls, and bottles like Roald Dahl's character the BFG (Big Friendly Giant, from the book of the same name), with his shelves full of bottles of dreams. Neither image is remotely close to the truth of course, but such small ideas help me remember to whom we belong, and by whom we are created.

EIGHT

Kept

SWADDLED

Like any loving parent, God desires to keep us held within the bounds of his love. He wants to hold us in love. As we recognize our smallness, we begin to understand that God keeps that compact, true, whole self that has dispensed with all unnecessary things. Such a small thing has become re-wombed in the heart of him.

Julian tells us, "God bases his judgement of us on our essential nature which he always keeps whole and safe with him; and he judges us in his righteousness."[1] There is a sense of space in this vision. The thing like a nut is utterly tiny, but it is not held in a clenched fist, but an open palm. It is seen and watched over, not grasped in ownership, though that might easily have been the case, but God does not keep his creation like a possession, like a pinned butterfly in a glass case of chloroformed universes, but in full view. He wants to watch it unfold, to give it room, to witness its being and becoming.

The picture of the hazelnut is preceded by an understanding of how God wraps us carefully and securely in clothing, so that the nut too becomes an image of such motherly swaddling. Julian uses the word *enfolded* several times, when she speaks of how we are kept in God's love. Our eternal soul is clothed in his love as the body is in flesh. His presence and tender care is in one sense the shell of the "nut," the belly of the womb, the hand around the nut and around the wound, the meniscus of the blood drop. The boundaries, the edges, hold us. We are held in love. Swaddled in it. Kept safe in it. It calls to mind the father wrapping the cloak around the prodigal son. It is an image of fatherly as well as maternal love, of grace and protection.

In the image that will come later to Julian of the Lord and his servant, the servant's garment is described as "threadbare—almost worn out—and looked as if it was about to fall to pieces,"[2] calling us back to the image of the nut that is also utterly fragile. Our outer, earthly, worldly selves, maybe our egos, everything about us that is mortal and impermanent, shows us its potential for demise when we recognize our smallness. It can be hard to see or acknowledge, but when we do, God's greatness and love can be more easily perceived.

The nut, or indeed us, is carried, held carefully and tenderly. If we hold something precious, we keep it in the palm of the hand. The soft vulnerable flesh in the center. This is how we swear oaths, placing our palms under our thighs (as in ancient Israel) or spit and shake hands, hold upright with one as the other lays on God's Word, the Holy Bible in court, or place on our hearts to pledge allegiance. The palm is connected to promises, to oaths, to the truth, and to the heart. It connects with the very center of all we hold dear. God says, "See, I have engraved you on the palms of my hands; your walls are ever before me" (Isaiah 49:16).

The palm is also a place of treasure and fortune, where our future lies, and some say may be read (by those who practice divination, not followers of Christ) who will ask us to cross their palms with coins of silver or gold. But if we are givers of alms, we might press a coin into the palm of a beggar's hand, that they might hold it well and keep it safe.

We hold our palms upwards in prayer, a sign of being open to God's presence, gifts, and goodness. A sign too of peace: when we show our palms, we are coming without weapons, open-handed. If our hands are empty and open, maybe our hearts will be more willing to listen too.

Again and again we are assured that the nut, that we, are kept and loved, coming back to the image of enfolding at both ends of this showing, likewise enfolding itself. The nut is clothed in God's love, in his hand. It is not smothered, but given space to grow and breathe. We might imagine too that being held in a circle of flesh, it is kept warm and comfortable, like an egg in a nest.

Because its fragility is emphasized such that Julian thinks it might disintegrate any moment, I always feel the nut is about to do just that, to break open like a chrysalis into a flight of color. Or perhaps given how it feels to Julian, this has already happened, and God is holding the remains of our earthly lives as deeply precious, just as he does with our tears and our brokenness. This might be especially so since Julian has just been so close to death.

Perhaps this holding of the nut is an image of the center of our suffering, merged with Christ's, or the beauty of our brokenness, left behind, and which no one but God will pick up as treasure. The nymph case of our developing selves, or perhaps the pellets we heavenly owls have formed out of discarded, unwanted things. Dried-up husks left behind, our testimonies, testaments to our transformation. Perhaps universes have grown and flown from this place, nurtured and incubated in the nest of God's hand.

God holds all stages of our larva-lives, our earth, and our universe as deeply precious. Since Julian calls him "eternity," perhaps this is a moment in time, akin to the crucifixion, when all seems lost, broken, about to disintegrate, become as nothing. And it is God who will smile over us, and breathe and call us into new life, just as when Christ breathes his last and turns everything on its head, becoming for a short time a corpse-cocoon ready to sit a while before cracking into a new self so bright his nearest and dearest can barely recognize him.

If we contemplate the fact that, as those who are made, we too are held within the small round thing, we might think about how it would feel to be enclosed or incarcerated. We might have had circumstances in our lives that made us feel trapped, caged, unable to move freely in the ways we would like. I would certainly say that my chronic illness and resulting disability has made me feel that way, imprisoned in a body that cannot do the things I would like it to. Many of us share, too, the experience of being trapped in a relationship of some kind that made us feel that way. Like we were in the dark, controlled, unable to move properly or be ourselves, held perhaps in the thrall, or even the hand of someone abusing their power over us. This happens in marriages, families, and even the church of course, as we all sadly know.

Perhaps we have also known the vice-like grip of depression, debt, or frustration, that powerlessness that means we cannot unfurl, or ever relax, or begin to develop into the people we know we could be. Unchosen material poverty does that as well, holds us fast and stops us moving in the direction we want to go.

So many things in life can make us feel in the grip of dark forces, clamped into small circumstances against our will. Childhood can feel that way too, often if we are neglected or simply feel no one is listening to us or helping us, because there are many things we cannot achieve on our own, or need permission to do; we can feel held back, as though our wheels are spinning beneath us and we are going nowhere.

There is also a kind of enclosure that can be chosen. Nuns and monks, friars and hermits choose smaller communities away from the world. A hermit or an anchoress often chooses solitude, and much of the day is spent alone in prayer in religious orders. Silence might seem to those outside such establishments as a kind of crushing limitation too, but many of us would say it was actually freeing.

There is a difference between choosing an anchored life as Julian did, or a cloistered life as so many saints have, and being trapped and frustrated in the dark. It is similar to the difference between poverty that is chosen, and that which is not. Saint Francis and Saint Clare spoke of choosing Lady Poverty, and gave up the rich blessings of financial comfort. They chose to live in poverty, to beg alms and work with their hands to support themselves and their communities in order to be like Christ and to follow his directives on money. They knew that to serve Christ they could not also serve mammon. It can sound like a kind of courtly ideal until the reality of lack and hunger hits. When we are trapped in poverty by circumstances, poverty is a lot less focused on the image of Christ or his teachings and becomes just another hard thing to bear.

Loneliness or unwanted seclusion, such as that suffered by the lepers of Francis's day, is something else entirely. I struggle with this, I admit, because I did not choose to be sick, or shut away, or lonely. The key difference for me has been acceptance. I've had to accept enclosure and poverty as my lot. Because I have given over my life to Christ, because I have given him my yes and asked him to let me be a living sacrifice, it has become as though I *had* chosen those things for love of him, and I can offer them up in a similar way to the saints and teachers I've so admired. In my small way, I can feel a kinship with Julian and with Clare (who was also sick and mostly bedridden in her later years).

I know that God could lift me out of sickness and out of poverty. I accept that up to this point and maybe for the foreseeable future he has chosen not to do that. Perhaps I need to be held to this stillness to do this work well. Perhaps if I were healed or granted a fortune, I might squander them on things that don't advance the kingdom. Perhaps I am so weak-willed and foolish that this is the best way I can serve my Lord. I cannot possibly know, therefore I must trust.

I trust that I am seen and known, in all my weaknesses and potential. I trust that the work set before me I can do, albeit in tiny slivers. I trust that this book is worth writing and, more importantly, will be worth reading. I trust my small, short life to God and ask for everything in it to be his and conform to his will. This is how we find ourselves, when we know we are small, when we know we are God's. We are made, kept, and loved.

When we understand that we are *held* in love, it makes all the difference. We know God is good and that we exist within infinity and eternity, however small and cramped things are now. However low our circumstances become, we know that we have a sure and certain hope. We are not held captive, but held, captivated.

When we understand where the tiny seed of our life sits and who watches over it, we will no longer be afraid. We then long to turn to his face, see the light, and begin to grow toward it.

When we come home after running away to the pigpen, we feel the softness of the velvet robes we thought were suffocating us, and we start to accept the loving embrace of the Father, God. Then we can let our heartbeat slow. We can relax, and realize we are home and beloved. Even if all seems dark and stifled, we are being held by, wrapped in love. We can accept that we are swaddled in a loving universe that will incubate and hatch us, birth us, let us break out, conspire with us that we might germinate into our true and naked, humble selves, and begin as new seed.

As we contemplate the hazelnut in the hand, with its crown and its stripes curving down the brown shell, we see that the way into creation and contemplation remains Christ, the wood, the cross, the heart, the crown of thorns and his stripes by which we are healed. All our potential and growth is held safely inside him. It is when the curtain tears the temple of us in two that we reach the seed, and begin our journey to becoming the tree of ourselves.

If we think on the crumbly and pale hazel kernel inside, we will not wonder at Julian thinking it might disintegrate. In some ways, once free of its outer coat, the hand then becomes the shell. Like all prophets we are granted a new mantle and the space to grow into it. We have been wooed into a spacious place free of restriction, and our encampment has become enlarged (Job 36:16; 1 Chronicles 4:10). We have room to see and grow and to become rooted and established in love (Ephesians 3:17).

Like Christ, we have been stripped of our protection. We lose the symbols of him, the cross ceases to be merely a metaphor, and we fall into the nail wound in the palm of his hand to become one with him on the very cross we have been contemplating.

The realization of our smallness that Julian is being shown is also where we discard all our protections and disguises. We let go of the safety and comfort of a world made to shape itself around us. We know we need to crack wide open in heartbreak and suffering to see things as they really are and know God's abundance. We no longer desire to take up all the space nor to remain in comfortable, familiar darkness. God's spacious places are calling us.

How else shall we be readied for the things of heaven but to have our perception changed? We cannot stay infants forever; we must hatch and grow. The old wineskin must crack. Teresa of Avila uses the image of a silkworm in its cocoon as an analogy for the soul that needs to be transformed before it can break out into new life. Once this happens, we might proclaim with Dorothy in *The Wizard of Oz* the truth that we have found a new, brightly colored world and are clearly not in Kansas anymore.

SAFE

It has always seemed to me that there is a lack of cohesive teaching on eschatology (what happens at the end of all things) in the church. There is a lot of popular fiction and conjecture about the rapture and the prophecies in Revelation, but not much solid, doctrinal work, or at least none that filters down to those without theological training like myself. It doesn't seem to be an area theologians are clear or consistent about in any way. And some might say, given the lack of clarity in the Bible, that this is understandable; yet there is more written on this than on other subjects which are given more houseroom. On what is our understanding of the end times really based? It is important when it is about mortality and immortality, about how our world will die and be reborn. *The Great Divorce* by C. S. Lewis gives us a good deal to think on about heaven and hell and is one of the best attempts to speak of all this I've seen.

One of the reasons people love Julian so much is that she really does push God on whether we are all going to be okay. She is seeking reassurance of grace, which she is not getting from church or itinerant preachers, but sees in Paul's epistles, and in the face of her Savior. She and everyone she knows have lost so many loved ones. What is their ultimate fate, then, if God is love as he must be and proclaims himself to be? And knowing her heart and ours, God keeps coming back to two things in his answers: that his meaning is love and that all shall be well. In other words, we can relax. Not into sin—the message of grace in Paul so powerful to those who've heard his preaching that he has to spell that out (1 Corinthians 6:12)—but into powerless love, being living sacrifices. Because this is a message to be received by those who love God or who will love God.

Julian's message is so similar to Paul's that she too has to issue a warning: "But if as a result of all this spiritual encouragement that I have spoken of, any man or woman were to treat sin lightly, or be foolish enough to say or think, 'if all this is true then it's a good idea to sin in order to get a better reward,' then beware! Should such a thought arise, it would certainly be a lie."[3] No, Julian assures us that while it is God's purpose to bring us into a whole new world of loving mercy, for love's sake we should abhor sin.

To the soul who has tasted God's mercy, Julian tells us he says, "My darling, I am glad that you have come to me. I was with you all the time in your trouble, and now you can see my love and we are united in happiness."[4]

We can be rather too eager to proclaim Julian a universalist. Yes, she had to be careful to state she believed the teachings of the holy church, but I don't think this was said just to protect herself. Julian was a truly devout person and would have known to query anything, whether seemingly given by God or not, that went against a lifetime's learning of doctrine. This was and should remain our plumb line when we read any text purporting to hold wisdom, or examine our own experiences of God. The Scripture and the central teachings of the church tradition must be expanded upon, never denied.

But Julian does have questions, and she is not afraid to ask them. She wants to know how far God's mercy will extend, what the grace of the cross will do, and what will happen when we die. And though God refuses to go into specifics, for there are things we cannot yet know or understand, I get the feeling that he is holding back in some sense because he does not want to spoil the surprise: "As the vision continued I understood that I was given it because of the great event still to come. . . . All this he revealed to me with great happiness, indicating that I should accept it faithfully and trustfully."[5] God is totally reassuring, telling Julian that he will deal with evil, sin, and every pain. We come away with the understanding that the cross has accomplished and continues to achieve a great deal more than we can imagine. We are right to put all our hopes there along with Julian and choose Jesus for our heaven.

Certainly, it makes sense for Julian to look to Christ, to the heaven she sought to enter through his grace, as her home or security. There was certainly no such thing to be found in her earthly life. She comes back over and over to the Middle English word *secker*, meaning safe or secure, because her life had been witness to wave upon wave of tragedy, most deaths by the plague being particularly sudden. She must have lost a lot of people dear to her, and likely would have carried worries about the eternal damnation of those taken without recourse to the last rites. As Julian scholar Veronica Rolf tells us, "That Julian uses this word again and again is a key into her character. It tells us what she wanted most, to feel safe and protected."[6]

Yet Julian was taking a great risk in writing at all. She could have been persecuted if she was indeed a laywoman, for writing a religious text or tract. She might have been accused of heresy or Lollardy (the preaching from or passing round vernacular translations of the Bible). As Rolf reminds us, "For any one of these infractions Julian could have been excommunicated, imprisoned or even put to death."[7]

Julian was also perilously aware of the paradox that you can have your eternal rest in God but that doesn't mean you will have security in this life. It is simply precarious to exist, even shut away from the world and all its ills. You are still a little nut that might crumble into nothing. But perhaps, like all of us, she was searching for sanctuary. What makes her so rare is that she was doing this, not just for her own sake, but to be somewhere she could ask God all these questions safely, process his answers and her own understanding, and pass them on to generations of *evenchristen*. She knew she wasn't doing this for herself alone.

All of us who have lived through struggles and heartbreak can empathize with Julian. Like her, maybe we all want sanctuary and *secker*, a place where we feel utterly secure, a safe place. Ultimately it is home that we are all searching for and hoping we can find in God and in his heaven. We wonder if he can be that for us. Julian says yes, he is the *only* place to find such a thing. This echoes Augustine, who told us, "Our hearts are restless until they rest in God."[8] Julian's vision of the hazelnut catapults her into the conclusion that God is the only safe place, and this understanding should compel us to pray her heartfelt prayer. He is the only home we can ever truly have. "For he," says Julian, "is true rest."[9]

Where could Julian find this place for herself in such a tumultuous life? Where can we, in our equally noisy, time-pressured, and uncertain twenty-first-century lives? Where is safety, sanctuary, but in a little nut boat in a shell in the safe walled harbor of God's hand?

In Julian's time, Norwich was a city walled on three sides, the fourth side adjoining the River Wensum. And while it was one of the safest places in England from invaders, it could not keep out the plague, nor the violence of war or religious intolerance. What it did do was give Julian an understanding of enclosure, and of man-made security. The idea of a harbor, and of anchoring, with the estuary and sea so close, and the city so secure, were certainly fixed in Julian's way of living. Walls, shells, enclosure, wombing, death, these things were everywhere, as were Julian's experiences as a woman with an intellect and spiritual depth that was frustrated by barriers to opportunity and education put up everywhere by patriarchy.

One of the truths that Julian's hazelnut showed her was that God "keeps us in his blessed love."[10] It seems an odd conclusion to many of us, when we look around and see so much suffering. God is keeping us, looking after us? And yet it is impossible, having seen what she has, for Julian to understand it any other way. God is goodness, is love, is devoted to loving and keeping us. Is God a safe place to be ourselves, become ourselves, without the world's unfair constraints, perhaps?

After receiving her revelations and the gift of the rest of her life, Julian chose a new path. We cannot be absolutely certain that Julian wasn't already enclosed when she received her visions, but there is accord amongst scholars that it is unlikely she was, given how many people were allowed around what they thought was her deathbed. Indeed Rolf lists her enclosure as being 1393 or 1394, twenty years after the revelations first occurred.[11] It seems much more likely that it was after this fulcrum point in her life that she decided to work toward entering the only place a fourteenth-century woman might become a writer, a mystic, a theologian: the cell of an anchoress.

Anchoresses weren't meant to teach or write but to pray for the town and dispense spiritual advice through a window onto the street. Julian was prepared to do this, but clearly had more in mind to achieve. She had so much on her heart about these visions, and more so, she had an idea of their importance and longevity, how they might comfort and be succor to a hurting world. She shared God's heart of wanting to comfort and reassure those terrified of being carted off to hell at a moment's notice.

To this end, Julian wanted to dedicate herself to learning better how to read and write, to set herself to the task of setting down all she had been shown. Most likely she had already made notes somehow or spent the intervening years with so much on her heart. She knew she needed quiet seclusion and some kind of stability to draw the truths out of the nut. Somewhere to plant it and let it grow. She had a depth of understanding that the fruits that would come were to benefit many. She set herself to becoming shut away so that her hazelnut might be held, *secker*, and allowed to germinate, become rooted and established both in Norwich and the love of its people, but especially in the heart of God for his dear ones.

Julian's saintly dedication certainly paid off for the kingdom of God. Although she could never know anything of it in her long life (records show she was still alive, aged seventy-one, in 1413 when Kempe visited; she likely died in 1416),[12] Julian's book eventually became a spiritual classic and has helped many thousands, if not hundreds of thousands of her *evenchristen*, in its unequivocal expression of the love and mercy of God through Christ Jesus.

At the coronation of King Charles III in May 2023, a specially commissioned rood screen was used for the sacred anointing of the monarch. On it was the embroidered image of a tree, and at the bottom, the immortal words spoken to Julian in her revelations, "All shall be well, and all shall be well, and all manner of things shall be well." There is no question that Julian's little hazelnut certainly grew! There is even an Order of Julian of Norwich based in Wisconsin, USA, which is a dispersed community with oblates and associates worldwide.[13]

SECURED

When we begin a deeper prayer life, we encounter some discomfort. No one wants to know they are empty or small, to feel that their worth might not be of their own making. We learn as we move along the contemplative path, which is perhaps more of a spiral than a linear journey, that our innate worth comes from being made in the image of God and from being beloved. That path too makes me think of Julian's or God's open palm, and the rhyme my mother used to say when I was a child, running her finger around the palm of my hand, "Round and round the garden, like a teddy bear, one step (to the elbow) two step (to the armpit), tickle you under there!" A sweet thing, but a reminder that our palms are sensitive places where our loved ones will connect with us. Parents may touch us tenderly there, but as we already noted, we also shake hands and make promises using our palms.

God, too, is touching us in the soft, tender places that connect us to God's parenthood and loving touch. As we listen to his voice, whether it comes through Scripture, prayer, or an inner knowing, we begin to comprehend that every gift, every good thing is from God, just as James tells us: "Every good and perfect gift is from above, coming down from the Father of the heavenly lights, who does not change like shifting shadows" (James 1:17).

God is in control. God knows what he's doing. God is good. God has the whole world (as we sing as children) in his hands. A very apposite song for us to remember when we think of Julian. Why is it so hard for us to welcome this truth as adults, when after all, it means we can indeed let go?

The world, the flesh, and the devil tell us all the time how important and special we are, but they neglect to tell us how or why that might be. And so at the same time they form the narrative that we take to heart about how useless we are. It is a double whammy that is constantly confusing, full of part truths that either send us searching for approbation or make us think we deserve more, sometimes both. All we end up with is disappointment.

If we take these things to God, we find they are both distortions of the truth. We all matter, because we belong to God, who made us, loves us, and keeps us. We are indeed all special. What we can't stand in our immaturity is that we are also all equal. Like James and John in Mark 10:35–41 asking Jesus for special favors in heaven, we desperately want a hierarchy.

These skewed views are gateways to the worst sins. They allow us to put ourselves and our puny imagined talents on a pedestal, thinking they elevate us above our fellows. This, even though any gift we have was given by God in the first place. As Jesus counsels the sons of Zebedee after their request,

> "You know that those who are regarded as rulers of the Gentiles lord it over them, and their high officials exercise authority over them. Not so with you. Instead, whoever wants to become great among you must be your servant, and whoever wants to be first must be slave of all. For even the Son of Man did not come to be served, but to serve, and to give his life as a ransom for many" (Mark 10:42–45).

Selflessness, *kenosis*, giving our lives up, all this is part of becoming Christlike. Instead, often we somehow think ourselves important not because we are his but because we believe we have either earned or deserve it. But God's love does not need to be worked for and we certainly did nothing to be worthy of it! God alone is good and worthy of praise and our tiresome toddler egos hate that.

We must come to understand, as Julian does, that we are worthless in the sense that outside of this love, this relationship, we are very, very little, and nothing we do can stand. We are so small, that we might even simply crumble to nothing. Julian would have agreed with the Spanish sixteenth-century Carmelite nun, mystic, and writer Saint Teresa of Avila, who said, in her famous prayer-poem "Nada te turbe" ("Let nothing disturb you"), "Solo dios basta"—God alone suffices.[14] Julian, two hundred years earlier, put it this way: "Nothing less can be enough for us."[15] Like Martha's sister Mary, these women of God understand how to do the one needful thing (Luke 10:42), which is to sit at the Lord's feet and gaze at love: "The soul of man always does what it is created for: it looks at God, gazes at God, and loves God."[16]

Only when we see this truth can we become "weak enough to use," as Dennis Lennon put it in his book of the same name. It is only (paradoxically) when we come to him in the fullness of our emptiness that God can use us. And we must be wise in our understanding of that word *use*, as author Liz Carter counsels us in her book *Valuable*.[17] God does not use us as though we were simply resources, or as though our whole relationship is based (as so many human ones sadly are) on what he can get from us, because we have nothing he needs. It is simply that he wants us to work with him in the creation of his kingdom. He loves us all the time and that never changes, nor does the degree alter, no matter how depraved we are.

Like a loving parent baking in the kitchen, he wants us to come and crack the eggs and stir the mixture, not because we'd do it well, but because he wants to spend time with us, to have us participate in the good things that will come out of the oven later on. And the more we understand this, and see our own limits, and his greatness, the more we want to offer him something of use. That turns out to be, really, just love. Like the Virgin Mary, the only thing we can offer back is our yes.

We are held by God whether we know or acknowledge it or not. We are anchored in him and one with his creation. When we practice contemplation, we eventually realize that we are becoming moored to one spot, the central point of love, God's heart, the cross of Christ.

In her anchorage, Julian might have felt a union with the little hazelnut that also needed to be held in place, rooted to the spot in order to grow. It would be easy to get carried away with the metaphor. There are worse things to drift off with. But Julian's life had to become utterly grounded. In her love and dedication to God she imitates Jesus' mother Mary by giving God her yes. She imitates her beloved Christ by humbling herself to a new smallness. He became a seed in a virgin's womb by the power of the Holy Spirit. Julian became a woman enclosed in stone, leaning against God's house. Like a hazelnut planted in the wound of Christ's palm, or nestled in his side, she chose to settle, sit, wait, pray, and grow, trusting the process, letting things be.

I feel anchored to my sickbed, very often. It can be overwhelmingly frustrating. But at the same time, I have hopes that I might be sharing in a small way something of this holy practice of becoming rooted and established in love, holding to God in prayer. Gazing on the crucifix and icons in my room, how can I truly feel anything but honored? I hope that some grace flows here and that a few of my words or prayers have inched the reign of God along a little, or blessed a heart. We are all so small, in the end.

Jesus, showing his love for us by sharing our smallness, ended up nailed to a cross. He submitted to being held in place, in desperate, torturous pain. When we find ourselves held to difficult or constricting circumstances, maybe we can gain solace by remembering we are mirroring his love. We hold fast to the God of love who has placed us where we are and given us the work set before us, even if that work is hard, or tastes bitter.

The image of anchoring, familiar of course to a woman who lived her whole life near a city port, is overwhelmingly one of safety. An anchor keeps us from moving into danger, stops us being at the mercy of the waves, tides, and currents. Human beings as well as ships need anchoring. If we are to grow, to find our way, we need a safe place, stability, a constant. Julian's overarching message in her writing about the hazelnut is that this safe place is God, and only God. Nothing else will do. She goes so far as to say that we must count all creation nothing, if we are "to love and have God."[18] To be at the very center of love, anchored to God so that there is nothing between us, this is true anchoring, true rest, true *secker*.

In the Gospels there is a sense that crowds are constantly drawn to Jesus. It is not just some kind of human charisma. He is the focal point of something. Things are changed at the center where he allows the kingdom of the Father God to preside. People are healed, forgiven, transformed, released. They are *sozo*, made whole. This truth followed Jesus all the way to the cross and beyond. People felt compelled to get to him. They took great risks to do so, like the woman with the issue of blood, or the Roman centurion. They were willing, as were two sets of brothers, to throw down their nets, cast aside their old lives and livelihoods, and follow him. They made sacrifices.

Everything this world said was worth more had to be understood to be nothing in comparison to him. The weeping woman gave up her dignity, and probably her dowry, pouring both over his feet. And this is where Mary of Bethany sat, gazing, as we try to do, at the one needful thing. Christ is our anchor. He is the point that holds our gaze, pierces our hearts at the same time as rendering them whole. He is the love of God poured out for us, the fulcrum point of human history. The center around which we cannot help but gyre. He is home.

NINE

Loved

Creation exists, Julian is told, "because God loves it."[1] Love is the cause of the whole cosmos. There is nothing outside of God's love. Everything exists through it, Julian is given to understand. Love is, in other words, the prime mover, the first motive, love is the reason we are here, and it is the thing that holds us here. Yet what is love?

These days the idea of divine love is not widely understood. Love is mostly mentioned in the sense of romantic love, or love for family and friends. It's often presented as something saccharine, something we fall into and can just as easily fall out of. But the kind of love that creates universes and plans eternity and sacrifices its most precious beloved for others? The kind that will run from heavenly perfection to earthly tedium, toil, and horror, and then give itself up to an undeserved, violent death for the sake of humanity? That kind of love is not spoken of much outside of the church. It is so wild and extraordinary that we should be shouting it from the rooftops. This love of God is so great, so immeasurable, so mysterious, it ought to preoccupy our every moment. The beautiful summation in John 3:16 remains the closest to expressing it in words we can start to understand: "For God so loved the world that he gave his one and only Son, that whoever believes in him shall not perish but have eternal life."

This love holds us utterly precious and beloved. We matter to someone. And not just anyone, but our Creator and the Creator of all things, designer of the universe, ruler of heaven. And Julian is being shown that knowing this should not make us proud or full of ourselves and our own importance, because if we see rightly and truly our own nature next to God's we will see ourselves as so small and weak as being about to disintegrate. Knowing that we in our smallness are so loved brings us to our knees. It floors us. The response to such love needs to be that we recognize everything compared to God is nothing, then run to him to find our home, our belonging, our true love.

Love is, of course, the central theme of Julian's revelations and her book about them. It is love that is being shown, described, taught, offered. In this way, Julian's book is another gospel. It is full of the good news that God is good. It tells us that despite our own wickedness and smallness, that because of God's goodness, he loves us. Love is the root cause, the originator and keeper of all things, including we human souls who have no right to be deemed so precious. As the psalms proclaim,

> When I consider your heavens,
>   the work of your fingers,
> the moon and the stars,

which you have set in place,
what is mankind that you are mindful of them,
human beings that you care for them?

(Psalm 8:3–4)

When Julian questions God about the difficult things in life, about sin and about Christ's Passion, about suffering and death, about hell, even, the answer always comes back as being centered around and explained by God's immense love. On the very last page of her long text, Julian reveals that after more than fifteen years of longing to know what God meant by giving her these revelations, she was answered: "Do you want to know what our Lord meant in all this? Learn it well: love was what he meant. Who showed it to you? Love. What did he show you? Love. Why did he show it? Out of love."[2]

The servant who represents Christ in the allegory Julian is shown later in her revelations has "a solid foundation of love," and later the Lord counsels Julian, "I am the ground of your praying."[3]

God's goodness is the thing from which all else flows, even our own prayers. Could we say his goodness and love are the same thing? Or perhaps that goodness is the noun, the *being* love, and love is the verb, that acts on it. Either way they must coexist. The world is full of evidence of the Creator's love. So much so that Paul tells us we have no excuse for missing it: "For since the creation of the world God's invisible qualities—his eternal power and divine nature—have been clearly seen, being understood from what has been made, so that people are without excuse" (Romans 1:20).

Everyday things can teach us about the nature of God, becoming treasures for those of us who contemplate. Even a nut is a sacrament, a treasure, a grace to be meditated on. It is a container of mystery and wonder. We sit with it and honor deep questions. Like a squirrel holding an acorn, we shake our heads at the idea that a whole tree—perhaps in time, a whole forest—might be inside this tiny shell.

Maybe as God holds us in his hand, we can imagine him gazing in love at us. We too are sacramental wonders, pearls of great price, dear ones to be treasured. Love is indeed his meaning.

By this love, because of this love, we are restored, Julian tells us, by God's "blessed Passion."[4] It would be wrong to imagine that Julian's conclusions about God's making, loving, and keeping us were anything but deeply trinitarian. The whole time we meditate on her words, we must keep in mind that she was seeing and understanding all she did at the same time as gazing at the image of the crucified Christ before her, both literally, in the crucifix held by the curate, and figuratively, as the visions of the Passion imprinted themselves on her sight, heart, and soul.

Our creation happened through Christ, God's love was shown us through Jesus' life and sacrificial death, and through that same act we are kept and restored. The Father, Son, and Holy Spirit are a constant, whole presence, working together to express love.

Many theologians would use the word *saved* rather than *restored*. The word the gospel writers use most often to mean both saved and healed is the Greek word *sozo*, which holds too a sense of being made whole. *Restored* seems a great translation of that to me. Jesus counsels us to make ourselves perfect, just as the father is perfect (Matthew 5:48). I'm sure I'm not the only one for whom this verse has been a bit of a stumbling block. But learning that the word he is using here for perfect is *teleios*, meaning complete, or whole, was a life-changing revelation for me, and I heard this during a short homily at Aylesford Priory. I hope to be well enough to return there one day, as it always felt like a spiritual home to me.

I wonder how frustrated Julian got at not being able to visit the cathedral or the river, and whether, like me, she would sit and use the power of her imagination to be in places of peace and beauty that she was no longer able to get to. Yes, she lived in a room annexed to a church, but we must all make our spiritual homes within ourselves. By this I mean that we are anchored to God, not to any specific place on earth. There are always particular locations and people that awaken our love of God and help us feel it more keenly, but when circumstances keep us tied down, we have to learn to carry those places and voices with us and tuck them up in our hearts so that we can ponder them as treasure, just as dear Mary did with all her memories.

It is within ourselves, too, that we begin this process of restoration. Things of heaven are almost always about process. Miracles are rare wonders, and it is in gradual change or growth that we are more likely to experience heaven on earth. We have epiphanies, moments where our perspective becomes clear and initiates huge changes, and seeing our own smallness over and over again is doubtless one such clarity. We often need to revisit such radical turning points and reevaluate where we are and what they have taught us.

Of course, the main thing we mean by God restoring us is the death and resurrection of Christ Jesus, by which grace we can receive eternal life. This is the Passion of which Julian speaks, and it informed the entire period of her revelations, gazing as she was on the crucifix. It is here at the center of all love, of all suffering, that we are "oned" with God, where our at-one-ment happens. Later on in her book, Julian describes how at the point of his death, a marvelous change overcomes Jesus' face, turning him from horrific suffering into utter joy, and that this instantaneous and miraculous transformation will be available to us too as we pass over death into life: "Just when I thought his life seemed about to end and his death was bound to be revealed to me, suddenly, as I looked, the expression on his face changed. This change in his holy face made me change, too, and I was as glad and joyful as could be."[5]

We are given this gift of Christ's Passion like a bridge, or a gate, allowing us to enter where we have no right, none of us being worthy to come to heaven. Yet through Christ we can pass over from this life into eternity. Reminiscent of Paul's use of "in the twinkling of an eye," in 1 Corinthians 15:52, Julian tells us, "Without a moment's break we shall pass from one state to the other and we shall all be brought into joy."[6]

As Jesus himself said to the criminal being crucified, "Truly I tell you, today you will be with me in paradise" (Luke 23:43). Heavenly love, then, is not just words, but actions. It is active in its passionate and compassionate feelings toward us. It stops at nothing to run and meet us where we are and to enter into our suffering with us. God's love is redemptive because it is boundless, it cannot help but rush in where angels fear to tread, and give everything up for its object. That we are the center of God's love, that we are the children tended to by this deep, abiding, suffering affection, is truly mind-blowing and heartrending. Love is who God is, and it is what he does. Our response is also love, such as we are capable of, and grateful awe.

GOD IS...

TEN

Heavenly

UNCREATED

It is vital to Julian's understanding of her shewings, as well as our own, that God is seen as separate from creation in the sense of having been the one who made it. Though Julian tells us that he is in it all, she is clear that he is also apart from it because he was not made. As detailed before, it's important to note that this is a panentheistic rather than a pantheistic understanding—that is, God inhabits creation and cares for it and is reflected within it, but is not contained there. We must always be able to differentiate the potter from her clay or the weaver from his threads. The one is greater than the other. As theologian Mark Oakley has said, "God is in the world as poetry is in the poem."[1] Indeed, the whole message of this shewing for Julian is that we must consider everything created as nothing, that we might begin to value God properly as so much greater.

God has made us and invested in us the highest possible worth, loving us to such a degree that he lowered himself to become very flesh amongst us and undergo the worst suffering of every kind. But he is also presumably quite able to create a billion more universes with every moment that passes. We are completely incapable of understanding God or what comprises God. We know from what Jesus told us that God is Spirit, rather than matter, and we perhaps understand this as some kind of vague, wispy, not quite solid thing. It seems gaseous or ethereal. But this is our ignorance showing, as ever. For what do we mere creatures entwined to mortal flesh understand yet of what eternity is made of, or what living outside of time really means? What is "forever"? We cannot possibly grasp any of it.

The apostle Paul tells us we are body, spirit, and soul (1 Thessalonians 5:23). We know that we believe in the resurrection of the body, but that it will take some new, incorruptible form, and we might perhaps discern that the soul (*psyche*) is our mind, our character, our heart, our personality, our whole "self," and that the spirit is the part of us that is God's breath, the *pneuma*, the sigh that he cannot let go, that will come home to him when we die. These are my own small wonderings, because much reading is beyond me, and I hope the reader will forgive me on that and look to the teachings that we are bound to within the Christian church. I believe that these three parts which make up our whole all go on in some fashion into eternity, but in renewed form. We will have a new body and a purified soul while remaining who we are in some way, and our spirit has always belonged to God and stands ready to return home to heaven with us in tow.

In chapter 45 of her *Revelations*, Julian is shown that even while we are on earth, our true self, the core of us, our dearest soul is held safe in God's heart: "God bases his judgement of us on our essential nature, which he always keeps safe and whole with him."[2] There is, then, nothing that can separate us from the love of God, as Paul is right to assure us (Romans 8:38–39).

Since Scripture tells us over and over, this life and its troubles are meant to shape us. All we go through helps us develop our characters, exists to allow the growth of the fruits of the Holy Spirit, who comes to live alongside us. Those very hard-won parts of us I think must be brought with us into our eternal lives. I believe this is why Jesus tells us that the kingdom of heaven begins right now, right where we are, that it is "at hand." We can begin to grow into our heavenly selves at any point, learning to become our *teleios* (whole and true) perfect selves, which is who we will be once we cross over into our new lives.

But for now, we understand that God is Spirit and relates to the Spirit within us, and that we are his creation. He is uncreated. No one made God. This is a sticking point for many atheists I know. But really this is just a failure of imagination on our part. We cannot think of something that was not made if we have never encountered any such thing. All that we know and see around us is made of matter, it is caused, quantifiable, observable in some way. But Spirit, we do not know. We cannot measure it or see it, we can only believe that it exists. But we can, I must say, sense it. Many millions of people have sensed the presence of God. We know that it is other, that it is something else, not of this world as we know it.

Beyond that, all we have experienced is God's creation. As we saw in Romans (1:20) earlier, Paul says that we all know that we live in a made universe, that it is obvious, and that we have no excuse for not believing that this is so. This will lead us to the belief, which some call ontological, that there must be a maker. But that he in turn is unmade is hard for us to grasp. God has always existed. No one begat or made God. He just is. This is fundamental to God's identity. This is why he calls himself "I AM," when Moses asks who God is in Exodus 3:14. He is loving presence. He is.

We spend our whole contemplative lives trying and failing to just *be*. Perhaps we instinctively understand that this is who God is. The ultimate being. Yes, he made everything, yes, he connects everything, yes, he loves everything. But there is no causality framing the existence of God. We understandably struggle with that concept, living as we do in a life where everything has cause and effect built into its systems.

For the same reason, we struggle with any way of comprehending existence outside of time, which presumably is what eternity is. There is no "before" God, because his existence is not linear. It seems to me that God had to create time ("there was evening and there was morning, the first day") because he knew we could not exist in a world that didn't have a system for containing our lives, our growth, or our becoming. Time was created as a womb for us to be held safely within, an eggshell, even a nutshell—perhaps to God as small and round a containment for a reality that looks to him as small as a hazelnut—and here is where humanity and all creation is kept safe and allowed to grow into what it needs to be before it can break out into eternity. All this is for our own good, I am quite sure, since God has deemed it necessary, and he does everything out of love.

And while I have said that God is capable of creating a billion universes in a heartbeat, Scripture seems to state that he has created and invested everything in this one small world in this one universe. It is entirely possible that this is simply to help us with our own weak understandings. If there are other universes or multiverses, or whatever else might be imagined, they are probably not for us to concern ourselves with when we ponder "all that is made." Our one small round thing is enough to think on for now. And yet I must say that I believe that even if there are other inhabited worlds, other places or lifeforms created by God, that they must all have their center in Christ. The cross, it seems to me, is so powerful and central a force of love, that it must be the cornerstone of everything.

In any case, no Christian, whether astrophysicist or science fiction writer, needs to countenance or indeed counter the arguments atheism brings, except to be ready with an answer when asked (1 Peter 3:15). Whatever we might come up with as theories or "supposals," we will find there is no ousting God from his rightful place as Maker of all.

In seeing all that is made, just as it is, Julian understands that she has no desire to possess it; she only wants to "have" or possess Christ the unmade Creator. As ever, creation points the way to God. It is a way, along with Scripture, of understanding who he is, of bringing us into longing for him, knowing he is our home.

Everything that is made must mean everything that is not God, since only God is unmade, and Julian immediately understands it includes her as an individual. She is keen to grasp what this seeing means to each of us. She jumps straight to her own restlessness, her own desire to be united with him. Julian longs for the made to be unified with the unmade, creation with its maker, even as she sees them separately. As we sense this longing with her, perhaps we sense God longs for this too. The Father runs out to the prodigal child, preempting our epiphany that if God is love, we can run home to his loving mercy.

ETERNAL

God is eternal—in fact, Julian says he is eternity. And yet he chose to create and clothe us with mortal flesh. I believe this means that we are in our seed form in this life. That the very small thing that is maintained by his love contains all our potential. We are currently perishable, yet when we die, as Paul tells us, those with faith in Christ will take on our immortal, imperishable forms (1 Corinthians 15:52). No wonder we look like tiny, disintegrating things to anyone looking at us from the eternal realms of heaven, because that is what we yet are. Rightly the writer of Hebrews echoes the psalmist, exclaiming, "But there is a place where someone has testified: 'What is mankind that you are mindful of them, a son of man that you care for him?'" (Hebrews 2:6).

God is mindful of us, cares for us, because he can see the entire timeline. He can see who we are, who we are becoming, and how that wholeness will fit us for heaven. God sees who each one of us shall be once time falls away and we become immortal. We are seeds, and God is the gardener. We are here to die and be reborn, to let our ears of wheat fall to the ground, crack open, germinate, let our outer layers disintegrate and our inner potential become rooted and established in love (Ephesians 3:17). Only then can we become all we are meant to be, united with our Maker. He sees this in us, and he sees everything we need to go through. We will call it pain, suffering, and sin, heartbreak, and agony. And it is all those things. But it is also the *via dolorosa* (way of sorrow and path to the cross) that we as triune creatures (body, soul, and spirit) must walk, if we are to come home to God.

Since God is eternal, I believe that time is a creation of God's and that he exists outside of its confines. Time is yet another swaddling cloth that has been instigated as a boundary to keep us safe. Just as infants are wrapped in tight cloths in many cultures to stop them kicking out and hurting themselves, so God has us held within the nutshell of time, of mortality, to keep us from bringing our eternal selves to harm. As we already mentioned, referencing Genesis 3:22 (see pages 62-63), this is also why we had to be expelled from the garden of Eden, so that we would not become unable to die in this state by eating from the fruit of the tree of life. Like everything that God forbids, it is for our own good, in this case, essential. For it was God who told the truth when he said we should surely die if we disobeyed him and gave up our innocence by eating the fruit of the knowing of good and evil, and the snake who lied by saying we would not. This is the long and painful path to heaven, coming home by dying, that the Lord knew we would take, and he had everything lovingly prepared. Our journey was always marked out in readiness, because our Father's sight and goodness is eternal. Julian reassures us of the passing nature of our suffering:

> After this God showed me a spiritual delight. I felt utterly full and sure of Him, strongly sustained without any feelings of painful dread. This feeling was so joyful in my spirit that I was totally peaceful and at rest and felt there was nothing on earth that could have upset me.
>
> This lasted only a short time. . . . God wants us to know that he keeps us secure and safe whether in happiness or suffering. . . . For it is God's will that we comfort ourselves with all our might: for our bliss will be endless, and pain is a passing thing that shall fade to nothing for those who are saved.[3]

ALL-POWERFUL

The heart of the message of this first revelation is that we must see our own smallness, fragility, dependence, and crucially, our insignificance, before we can find our rest in God. We have to see with an eternal perspective. Again, the connection with Mary is of great importance. It is because of her humility that she is able to say yes to God, even though what she's being told seems impossible. She trusts him absolutely because she knows her own smallness and powerlessness. If we imagine ourselves of any importance in and of ourselves without God, then we are not going to be able to join with him in any real sense. Jesus said both that we could do nothing outside of him (John 15:5) and that nothing was impossible for God (Luke 1:37).

Indeed Mary's hymn of praise to God after receiving her mission from the angel Gabriel, which we call the Magnificat (Luke 1:46–55), is a paean to this truth, that the Lord our God honors the small, the poor, the lowly, and that it is to him that all power and glory must be and should be given. We too must come to that conclusion, and Julian makes no bones about it: "We need to understand how small creation is and to perceive everything that is made as nothing, before we can love and have God who is unmade."[4]

It can be a hard place to find, this understanding that all our efforts mean nothing on their own. This is especially true for those of us brought up in cultures with work ethics, or meritocracies, where we are taught that we can become upwardly mobile, in a social and economic sense, if we just try very hard. I'm guilty of falling for that one with my writing and art sometimes. If you just keep persevering, the author narrative goes, eventually you will succeed! But it's not necessarily true. It might be yet another story that we are telling ourselves. We may not be very talented, we may write or paint in a style that's simply not in vogue during our lifetime, our work may not appeal in some subjective way to the agents or publishers we approach. We may not have the connections that are needed. Sometimes it doesn't matter how hard we try, the breaks are just not forthcoming. The same goes for almost anything in life. There are a lot of barriers to what we might deem "success." Being told we can achieve it by trying puts a lot of extra pressure on us, and encourages us to heap it on ourselves too.

For most of human history, and for most people alive today, success remains a matter of surviving the day well. It's about access to clean water and a meal, more than one if we are fortunate. People in Julian's day would have understood this better than we do in the West now. We can truly do very little for ourselves. We cannot even add one hour to our own lives, as the Lord teaches us. Not even by worrying! I am exceptionally good at worrying, so this is a bit of a blow to me.

It might sound counterintuitive to our striving systems and push-harder work ethics, but actually, realizing that someone else is in control, and it isn't us, is very freeing. Looking at Julian, living in such a time of seeming chaos, when the plague might take by nightfall someone you were talking to at market in the morning, it might seem odd to us that it was possible to even believe in God, let alone a good God, and let alone one who could proclaim that he would "make all things well."

Maybe it is harder for us, we who can (in theory at least) order food or a sound system to be delivered the next day, to believe that we need to give up our illusions of control and power. We seem to be doing pretty well, thanks. It is not until we are hit by a tragedy, a family death, or a serious illness that we realize just how changeable life can be and how little we can do about it. "Thoughts and prayers" have become what we feebly offer in times of crisis. Both are doubtless valuable. Solutions and healing are harder. Humility even more so.

Can we hand it all over to God? Can we believe that there are ways to work with him, to improve our lives and world, if only we knew how to let go of our selfish ways and admit that he is the best person to hold the world in his hands? We might shake our fists at such a Lord and wonder what he is playing at, as we witness all this suffering and calamity. This is always our human response to our own powerlessness. We could sort it all out if we were in charge and had cosmic, unlimited power, of course, and it would look very different from how God is doing things. It would never occur to us that the world and our own lives, to some extent, were in a miserable state precisely because we, both individually and as the human race, hadn't allowed God to reign in them. We might doubt, as Voltaire's eponymous protagonist Candide did, that we live in the best of all possible worlds.

Julian knew that this was how most people felt too. It was why she kept asking God the difficult questions during her revelations and why God kept answering her with such loving, gentle patience. For it is not only our rest that we find in God, but our peace and our meaning too. We seek answers to assuage our doubts and difficulties, and God is constant in his assurances to Julian. All shall be well, and everything is driven by love.

It is perhaps only when we look into that suffering, bleeding dear face of Jesus Christ crucified, that we finally have no recourse to fist-shaking and complaining. For who in the world ever suffered more? And as Julian and every other mystic and theologian who has seen or contemplated the Passion tells us, there was more loaded onto Jesus in this crux point of all humanity's suffering than we could possibly comprehend. "For just as he was the most tender and most pure of all people, so he was the one who suffered most deeply and intensely. He suffered for the sin of every man who is going to be saved; and grieved for every man's sorrow and desolation, with natural sympathy and love."[5]

In addition to carrying his own physical suffering, the crucified Christ also carries the world's pain. Not only that, but our sins too. Indeed, Julian even comes to comprehend sin as suffering, understanding it as both contrition and a gap that we need to have filled by love and mercy. If we can look here, we shall see our own pain and suffering, our own brokenness and inadequacy, being held and loved. If this is what holding all the power in the universe looks like, maybe it is in the best hands and it is good that they are not ours!

ELEVEN

Holy

TOTALLY WISE

God's wonderful qualities of goodness, omnipotence, and wisdom all work together as love. This message runs throughout Julian's book, that love is his meaning and everything cooperates to the best end. In proclaiming God totally wise, Julian is reminding us that we know nothing. Just as the small round thing is as nothing compared to God, so is all that we know in comparison to what God understands. His thoughts are so far above ours: "As the heavens are higher than the earth, so are my ways higher than your ways and my thoughts than your thoughts" (Isaiah 55:9).

When, like Julian, we are beset by both troubles and questions, God's answer is that we see our smallness and own it. We need to see who we are compared to the I AM. To some, this answer feels difficult, as though it were shirking the deep pain of those crying out for a reply. But this is to misunderstand. We ask God to explain himself, and he gives us himself. We want to know why, and he says *I AM why*. God himself is the answer. Few people in the Bible suffered more than Job, and he was also eager to ask God for answers. This is why he comes at Job out of the whirlwind with a torrent of truths about who he is as Creator and maintainer of the world, and forces Job to admit he is nothing in comparison: "You asked, 'Who is this that obscures my plans without knowledge?' Surely I spoke of things I did not understand, things too wonderful for me to know" (Job 42:3).

This is, actually, deeply reassuring. It's not an exercise in knowing our place, keeping us oppressed, but showing us we don't have to worry about anything because it is all in God's hands. We can't make the sun rise, or the snow fall, or keep the tide from overstepping its bounds. God has already taken care of all that. How much more then, as Jesus explains, will the Father know how to take care of the small things (Luke 11:13).

Of course, the Lord speaks to each one of us in different ways. To Job, in what is one of the earliest religious texts in the world, the encounter is strong and stark. Yet maybe that is what Job needed to hear, spoken majestically how he (and his "comforters") needed to hear it. It is also worth noting that God speaks poetically, in forms much like the Psalms. We cry out to him, he cries back to us.

For Julian, the answers seem gentler: "The answer came," and "I was answered," in short, easy-to-grasp sentences. God speaks to her as he did to Elijah, in that small, still voice, that gentle whisper that underpins everything.

If we have true perspective, we can see that the world is nothing, God is everything. This is perhaps easier to see if we have had everything cleared from our lives until only the basics remain, if we have undergone tragic loss, or if we have had the time to make prayer the center of our existence. In the hustle and hurry of the working, parenting, caregiving week, we can feel overwhelmed by the reality of pressing concerns, of both our needs and those of whom we love. No one has more compassion on that than God. Jesus speaks directly to the heart of the matter when he counsels us not to worry, saying, "But seek first his kingdom and his righteousness, and all these things will be given to you as well" (Matthew 6:33). It is what we place at the center of our lives that matters.

While there is very little we can truly grasp, we can believe and know that God is far beyond us in every way. If he created us out of his goodness, power, and wisdom in love, then we don't need to fret, nor question any of those qualities. We can be assured that everything is taken care of, understood, planned, underpinned. We can see that the everlasting arms are under us and that we are held carefully in the palm of God's hand.

Julian is given to understand still further that there is nothing done that is not done by God. He is the only actor:

> For I saw that God truly does everything, no matter how small. And I saw truly that nothing happens by chance or accident, but by the foresight and wisdom of God. If we think it is chance or accident, it is because we cannot see the truth. For the things that God anticipates by wisdom since before time (which rightly and to his glory he constantly brings to their best end) seem to catch us suddenly and unawares, and so in our blindness and short-sightedness we say, 'this is just down to chance.' But to our Lord God this is not the case.[1]

If we brought this utterly into modern parlance we might say that Julian is telling us we are wrong when we say, "That's just the way the cookie crumbles," and so on. God leaves nothing to chance. This is a tough truth, hard to comprehend. I do not believe God means by this that we are mere puppets to his schemes, but that he knows exactly what will happen, exactly what each of us, so entirely known as we are, will do out of our freedom, so that the prime actor, God, is like someone who has created a universe full of dominoes, and at his merest breath, they fall and continue to work toward the pattern and purposes he has foreseen. If this is a hint of what he means, then we should be glad and thankful that he is totally wise, good, and loving in his omnipotence.

GOOD

Lately I've read or heard a lot of people telling us that humankind is good because God proclaimed us so in Genesis after looking over all his new creation with gladness (Genesis 1:31). If God says we are good, it must be true, we are told. Yet when Jesus was called "good," he asked, "Why do you call me good?" And then he said, "No one is good—except God alone" (Mark 10:18).

This seems to contradict our current sermons. Perhaps this too is all about perspective. Ours ought to be that we are nothing in comparison to God. When prophets in scripture pronounce us to be "filthy rags" (Isaiah 64:6) or "worms" (Job 25:6), they mean in comparison to our Maker. We are "good" only in the sense of our being part of creation, which is pleasing to God. Only God is innately good.

What is this holy goodness? It is benevolence, selflessness, loving-kindness, and mercy. It is *hesed*, a Hebrew word used in

Scripture for a loyal and persevering love. It is *towb*, meaning pleasant, agreeable, beneficial, beautiful. God is without sin, it is impossible for him to do anything wicked, of course. But God's goodness is not defined so much by what it isn't, but by who he *is*. His whole character is about goodness. The psalmist counsels us, "Taste and see that the LORD is good; blessed is the one who takes refuge in him" (Psalm 34:8). Even when we are at rock bottom, in the pits of despair, we can still see and take comfort from the fact that God is good. One of my very favorite verses in the Bible is at the end of Jonah's short book. The prophet, though he is angry at God, still has to admit that the unchangeable goodness of the character of the Lord was what he was running from: "He prayed to the LORD, 'Isn't this what I said, LORD, when I was still at home? That is what I tried to forestall by fleeing to Tarshish. I knew that you are a gracious and compassionate God, slow to anger and abounding in love, a God who relents from sending calamity'" (Jonah 4:2).

It would be a terrible thing indeed if God were all-powerful but not wholly good. Thankfully we know from scripture that God is good, that he is holy. The honor, power, and the glory need to always go to him because he is the only one capable of using these things for good, and the only one able to wield true virtue and holiness. We are only made pure through his love, it is his sacrifice that cleanses us, nothing out of our own selves can make us good, wise, or holy. God gifts us sanctification through the sacrifice of his beloved Son, and this is where we find our rest.

If we brought together into a pointe all the poisonous sin of the world and let drop on it one molecule of God's love, which is the blood of Christ, it would be like letting an ocean fall on a grain of sand. Not because our sins are not manifold and grievous but because that is how pure and powerful and great is the mercy of God.

Once we comprehend in our smallness that only God is good, we long for him and can find our satisfaction nowhere else. Everything in us longs and prays for unity with the one who made us in his image. It is our yearning for home that brings us to his heart through Jesus. When we have this longing and see ourselves for the small, weak, fragile, sinful creatures that we are, we can then understand enough to speak the prayer which Julian describes at the end of this passage. It is another version, if you like, of the sinner's prayer, "Lord Jesus Christ, Son of God, have mercy on me, a sinner" (which we extrapolate from Luke 18:13), because it acknowledges our need of God and comes before him asking for nothing less than his best, his mercy. We ask him for the one needful thing, himself.

TRIUNE

Julian's writing constantly reflects and emphasizes the triune nature of God. So many turns of phrase feature three things, three qualities. The Trinity for her comprises love (the Father), joy (Christ), and bliss (Spirit). There are three degrees of bliss, three heavens. She even asked for three wounds. Three within one is the image of wholeness. Chapter 58 particularly takes us deeper into this knowing: "Our whole life consists of threes: first our being, second our increasing, and third our fulfilment."[2]

It is rare to find spiritual writings that encompass this knowing of God as three-in-one so naturally. It is a clear sign to me that Julian is steeped in prayer, in a deep relationship with God, even at the starting point of her revelations. She has met God and knows him as Trinity: "God the holy Trinity, who is everlasting being . . ."[3]

Julian knows that in gazing at the cross she is experiencing the mercy of the Father through the sacrificial love of the Son by the power of the Holy Spirit. The relationship and union of the three is accepted and understood. When Julian chooses Jesus for her heaven, it is partly because she understands this crucified Christ to be the perfect expression of trinitarian love. The heartbreak of the Father, the sacrifice of the Son, the workings of the Holy Spirit are all here, encapsulated in One love, with Mary, John, and the female followers looking on and participating in his pains. The cross is the focal, central point of love's song. It is where all is worked out and given up.

The cross is where God meets us. It is why we Christians hold it as our central symbol, our most holy image. In Julian's understanding, our union with God can only come through Christ:

> And our substance is in our Father, God Almighty, and in our Mother God, All-wise, and in the Holy Spirit, All-goodness. For our substance is whole in each person of the Trinity, which is one God. The earthly part of us is only in the second person, Christ Jesus, in whom is the Father and the Holy Spirit. In him and by his might we are brought out of hell, and out of the wretchedness of earthly life, brought up to heaven and blissfully united to our whole essence.[4]

In the vision of everything that is the tiny hazelnut, Julian comprehends the triune majesty of God over creation, for he is the one who makes, keeps, and loves it. The almighty, the all-wise, the all-good is our God.

TWELVE

Home

OUR REST

Rest—what it really is and where we can find it—is one of the main themes of the revelation given through the hazelnut. Julian mentions it a number of times, so that the repetition is quite striking. She mentions it as an aim in life alongside joy, and as the outcome of union with God: "for until I am totally united to him, I will never have total rest or true bliss." It is not only our delight but God's too, as "it pleases him when we rest in him."[1] Rest seems to be synonymous with peace, and that deep, meaningful, sabbath rest that is not so much about being carefree but being in a place where we can utterly trust that we are safe and loved.

We find our rest, even as small, disintegrating beings, fragile and broken, in the palm of God's hand. In the wounds of Christ, we lie; small, round as the head of a rusty nail. We are home.

God is true rest because once we have grasped our own insignificance, we can run to him knowing that we have no control or power over anything (that to think or feel otherwise is a delusion). We can very happily hand over our lives, giving ourselves (body, soul, and spirit) to God as living sacrifices knowing it is good and right for him to be in charge. Indeed, since he is anyway, all we are doing is acknowledging the truth. In this way we can experience great relief. A weight is lifted from our shoulders when we realize that we don't have to meet our own needs and take care of everything by ourselves, that God will see us and the world redeemed, that all is in his hands. Likewise, we can hand over our sins and suffering and weaknesses, our very selves on his altar, understanding something of the power of the grace of Christ. "Therefore, I urge you, brothers and sisters, in view of God's mercy, to offer your bodies as a living sacrifice, holy and pleasing to God—this is your true and proper worship" (Romans 12:1).

Our freedom, our rest, is in joining with our one true love and it is not that we won't suffer any longer, but that our suffering is united with his and has a purpose. This is all for the glorification of God, the redemption of his creation; but also when we realize this, we then know that pain is temporal and joy is eternal. Like Christ, we may begin to suffer gladly, which is to look at heavenly things with an earthly sight and to look at earthly things with our heavenly sight. God is in charge. In the ninth revelation, Jesus says to Julian, "It is a perpetual delight to have suffered for you. If I could suffer more, I would."[2]

Our true rest in God is not something we achieve, it isn't something we arrive at by our own efforts. If anything, the opposite is true. We come to a place of rest in God by receiving it. We see our own lack of security, peace, and rest, and must come to God knowing that we want it (in both senses). He longs to give us that rest, but can only do so, the same as with his amazing grace for our sin, when we can see that it is only God who can provide it.

RESTORER

When I think of God as restorer, I cannot help but imagine a master artisan, a craftsperson restoring an old painting, perhaps lifting off old layers of varnish to reveal the true picture beneath. God's restoration might be like that, as he brings us all to perfection, making everything right.

Throughout her book, Julian speaks of salvation as an act of being lifted up, as though we in our sin were simply dear children that need to be caught up in their mother's arms, or beloved servants that only tripped and fell in our haste to do our Lord's bidding. It is as though we have found ourselves in this position of needing redemption almost by accident. Julian tells us that there is no real desire to sin in us and certainly no wrath in God. Both of these things surprise her, seeming to clash with what she has been taught, until she wisely decides to hold both in a balance, knowing so many spiritual truths are deeper and more paradoxical than we are able to comprehend: "So this was my longing: to understand from God in what way the teaching of Holy Church is true in his sight, and in what way I can know it to be true; and how both judgements can be held together in a way that brings glory to God and seems right and consistent to me."[3]

There is very little in Julian about judgment. In fact, she speaks of God telling her that there will be not one, but two wonderful mysteries of grace that will happen which he cannot say more about, for none of us would be able to understand them. One will happen as we enter heaven, and the other later: "This deed and the one mentioned earlier are not the same, but are quite distinct. The one we have just discussed will happen first, as each of us comes into heaven. . . . But the great deed referred to earlier will not be known until it is accomplished—not by heaven, nor by earth."[4] Mercy's mysteries await. Something that should give us all hope.

It is in Julian's understanding of salvation and grace that we see most clearly her familiarity with the Bible, despite not owning one to study (this would have been incredibly unlikely, more so since she probably didn't read Latin). I agree with Sister Mary Paul (a Sister of the Love of God), who tells us that *Revelations of Divine Love* is clearly written by a person familiar with the New Testament, especially those parts written by Paul and John.[5]

Despite seeing the actual devil (who attempts to choke her) and two of his demons immediately after her visions, causing her to almost lose both her healing and doubt her revelations, Julian speaks little of the fires of hell. This is strange too for someone who must have been surrounded by illustrations and depictions of such things in mystery plays and medieval art. God's love is more real to her, and so deep that she knows evil is laughable in comparison. Heaven pours sweet love on our smallness and powerlessness, but scorns the same things in God's enemies, for we seek to come home to holy heaven, and they to stop us: "I saw the Lord scorn the devil's malice, and reduce his empty power to nothing; and he wants us to do the same."[6]

Restoration, salvation, to Julian by the end of her contemplations, is not about assuaging a wrathful God who would otherwise need to punish us, but about an outpouring of grace and love so strong and vivid, that it causes the blood of Christ to run as copiously throughout her text as it did all through her visions. "During the whole time that our Lord showed my spirit the vision which I have just described, with my physical eyes I saw heavy bleeding from the head," she writes.[7]

Because of this love she has to conclude that even all our wickedness, sin, the fall, and our suffering will serve simply to allow us to be lifted higher into God's heavenly kingdom love than if we had never fallen. She writes, "I saw with utter certainty that just as our sinful nature gives us pain, shame and sorrow here on earth, as it should, so grace brings about solace, worship, and bliss in heaven that surpasses all our earthly woes. So much so that when we rise and receive the sweet reward grace has brought about for us, we shall thank and bless our Lord, endlessly rejoicing that we ever suffered."[8]

The message she shares with us is that everything serves God's love for us and that all ailings can be turned to our good by his grace, that indeed, "You will see for yourself that all manner of things shall be well."[9]

When Julian tells us through her writing about the hazelnut that God has "restored us by his blessed Passion,"[10] she is telling us that it is Christ's suffering that redeems us, that calls us into being one with him. When we are sanctified and brought over from death to life by Christ's blood, we become united not only with our essential selves, but with Christ himself. The main act of the cross is one of suffering love and the effect of this is to restore us to God's arms, lift us up, make us one with our Maker. It is union, "oneing," that is the result of our restoration and another large theme within the *Revelations*: "Out of him we have all come, in him we are all enfolded, and towards him we are all journeying."[11]

LOVE

Even though love is the center and reason for all the rest, the why and how of our being made and kept and redeemed, it is the aspect of God that the majority of us struggle with the most. In a world where we suffer, many simply cannot believe that our Creator can love us. We certainly can't accept that he loves us in the lavish, abundant way we are told about through scripture, or by saints and preachers.

This problem of sin and pain in the creation of the Holy One is a question Julian asks God over and over during the revelations. The urgency and perseverance with which she continues to press God on these things that trouble us and keep us from believing in God's goodness are remarkable. Julian even balks herself at how hard she pushes, but it is as if she understands that we are all with her, urging her to find out for us. She seems to grasp that this is her chance to find out the answers to the questions that stop all of us in our theological tracks. If she doesn't ask now, when she can, while the door is open, so to speak, and while she is deeply aware of God's kindness and friendliness, then when might she?

Julian is not able to accept anything other than full answers now after all the wickedness and pain she has witnessed and undergone in her life. So she asks, and the answer that she is given over and over again is love. The knowledge of God's faithful, merciful love permeates the whole book. Its sweet fragrance rises from every page to bring us solace. "Do you want to know what our Lord meant in all this? Learn it well: love was what he meant. Who showed it to you? Love. What did he show you? Love. Why did he show it? Out of love."[12] Love was indeed his meaning.

In the end, it is the cross that answers both the question of why there is sin and why there is suffering. Julian finds all her answers in the crucified Jesus, whom she has chosen for her heaven.

All our rushing and stumbling in life leads to falls, just as it does for a toddler or an overeager servant running to please his master. Perhaps we might include even the falling we do in running away from our duties, as we see in the book of Jonah. Our falling is inevitable and in Julian's reading, it is also astonishingly expected, planned for, and completely forgiven. We are exonerated as though all we had done was fallen in a deep hole. God only wishes to lift us out, dust us down, and set us on our way.

As all Christian mystics do, Julian sees that God is good and therefore there is nothing to be done but praise and trust. Teresa is right, nothing need disturb us. "What can man do to me?" the Psalms and the writer of Hebrews ask, likewise (Psalm 56, 118; Hebrews 13:6). And although I'm often tempted to say, well, quite a lot, actually, we can look to Paul's assertion in his second letter to the Corinthians that any earthly suffering may be considered "light and momentary troubles" (2 Corinthians 4:17). If I challenged him on that, I'd be heckling a man who'd been beaten almost to death, shipwrecked, imprisoned, and vilified. In any case no one could beat the ultimate Pauline heckle of falling out a window to one's death during one of his sermons. Paul brings Eutychus back to life and then carries on preaching, by the way (Acts 20). All preachers need a good heckle, now and then, incidentally, just as all writers need editors. We all need to be wise enough to have people in our lives who keep us anchored to the earth, to our cross, to our truth, to this incarnation. Cats are useful for this too, keeping us in our proper place.

But in the end, none of this earthly pain, sin, or suffering will counter God's grace. As we've seen, Julian seems to have understood that these things will only increase our joy in heaven. As Paul finishes his sentence about troubles, he tells us that they are "achieving for us an eternal glory that far outweighs them all" (2 Corinthians 4:17). We can trust that God's love is so great that we, small as we are, powerless as we may be, so wicked as to be ever about to fall into nothing, need fear no ill. Julian too, reassures us of God's loving purposes:

> He will give us grace to love and cling to him. For he gazes on his heavenly treasure on earth with so great a love that he wants to give us more light and solace in heavenly joy by drawing our hearts to his from out of the sorrow and darkness we are in. . . . And I saw most certainly that before God made us he loved us with a love that never abated, nor ever shall. And all his works have been done in this love. In this love he has made all things good for us, and we shall live eternally in this love.[13]

This love is not a long-distance affection, viewing us down its nose from a great throne. This love runs to us with outstretched, bleeding arms. This love willingly, even eagerly, stepped out of eternity into the swaddling clothes of time and infancy. It passed from infinite freedom into the close, vulnerable, bloodlined womb. A mighty oak squeezing itself back into a crumbling acorn. A spreading mustard tree into a tiny speck-seed. An ancient hazelnut tree into one infinitesimally tiny nutshell.

Love sees our pain, love runs to us, love throws itself into the fire to rescue us, will stop at nothing to bring us back into the safety of its arms. After reading Julian, we can say with Paul, "For I am convinced that neither death nor life, neither angels nor demons, neither the present nor the future, nor any powers, neither height nor depth, nor anything else in all creation, will be able to separate us from the love of God that is in Christ Jesus our Lord" (Romans 8:38–39).

Conclusion

Julian teaches us that we gaze upon Christ crucified to know who loves, makes, and keeps us. We then begin to see and understand our smallness and our insignificance next to that of God, realizing we are nothing in comparison. This is *kenosis*, death of self, recognizing the fragile, mortal state of our existence. We wonder how we survive, why we don't crumble into nothing, shrivel up and die. When this truth hits home, then and only then can we recognize God's glory and our need for him and him alone, and find our rest and true happiness in him.

Sometimes I feel sorry for myself in my sickness and enforced seclusion from the world. I think of Julian and complain to God because I think she chose her solitude, and I did not. I wanted children, a career, to make a difference in the world. I wanted to be part of a church family and a community. I still do. I want to walk, see people, commune with nature, and spend time with my amazing husband. I miss films, TV, chats that are longer than a few precious minutes. These are all things I cannot do because I have no energy, since this illness has sucked away any ability to make it, as though my batteries are always almost, but occasionally not quite, dead. I am living a non-life, existing, not doing more than surviving. It hurts. I feel broken, let down, lost, disheartened.

And then I remember.

God is good. God is beyond us and yet intimately with us. God is uncreated Creator of all, totally wise, all-powerful, and eternal. God is loving mercy and kindness. God is to be worshiped and praised. God is holy and full of grace. I love him and he loves me. He is love. He loves everyone and everything. God is a safe place to bring all my questions and hurts. Julian shows us that is true, even if we take nothing else from her writings.

Even in the midst of locutions, revelations, and visions, Julian feels secure enough in God's love to ask all the questions that she feels she's never been able to ask before. And she finds answers. Some are simply framed as God knowing best. But as for Job, it is the encounter with the loving God that really provides the answers that he and Julian can trust. That you and I can trust. Once we know that God is good, that he has our best interests at heart in all things, then we can relax. We can trust, we can obey, we can be, knowing all is (both literally and metaphorically) in hand.

Any of us set aside, taken into a different or cloistered way of living, are set aside for a reason. Everyone we love, we love with the love of Christ and by the grace of God. There is nothing that the world could offer us back that compares with the worth of that pearl of great price. Julian even entombed herself with this treasure in order to consider it all her days. But God's compassion will not allow us to be completely cut off from the world. We must continue to partake of its woes and Christ's suffering. Otherwise, we cannot learn to love well. So even our "hiding" away is not that, nor should it be in any cloistered life.

Julian had her maids, her window where she offered spiritual direction and advice, and her window through the door into the church where she received the eucharist. She also had her writing, which she trusted was connecting her to her fellow *evenchristen*, though she could not have had any idea of the longevity of her words.

If we are set apart by God, having discovered this is his will for our lives, we might see it as creating a space to sit at his feet. If this were purely for our own benefit it would be a selfish act, but instead it becomes an act of love. It is a hard thing to do, one of many ways to become a living sacrifice.

Part of an anchoress's work was to intercede for the village or town that she lived in. So those of us who are in religious community or enclosed in any way spend a long time praying for others. In many ways our solitude makes us more connected to the world's needs, not less. A hazelnut tree, growing in one place, anchored to the spot, can never move; it is utterly invested in the conditions of the soil and air around it. Its roots run deep. It connects to the mycelium, the water table, and the mulch which surround it and to the weather that moves past.

Like Julian, I long to bless the world with my writing. Most of it is written, like this book, to draw people deeper into God's heart, into contemplation, and hopefully be comforting and encouraging to my *evenchristen*.

When the publishing world frustrates me, or readers are few, when completed books seem to be rattling round unwanted on my hard drive like lost hazelnuts, I think of Julian and how she had no idea that the writings she left behind would still be blessing us over six hundred years later. I do think she had some idea and a very real hope of her work being a blessing, else she should not have spent the greater part of her life praying over and finalizing them. She knew the revelations were for all of us and continued to have faith in that. It was a hope that kept her going.

This hope is mine too, for the moment, though of course on a much smaller scale. Julian is a master theologian, a wonderful spiritual teacher. Her one small book is full of treasured knowledge that we can dive into again and again and always find something new. As I write I have no idea if this small thing about just one of her shewings will bless or encourage anyone. I am simply sure that it is what God wills me to do at this time. Like Julian, I shall believe that "in all things God works for the good of those who love him, who have been called according to his purpose" (Romans 8:28), and that eventually, whether one or many read our words, it is who we are and to whom we belong that matters, and not our striving or doing. Whatever we leave behind us, we can trust that "all manner of things will be well."[1]

The key to this contemplation is that we will need to sit a while, in the palm of God's hand, to get our bearings. It is here where we will receive the knowing of our true size, the shape of our beginning, before we can start our journey into the space around us by growing, by reaching instinctively toward the light with all our inner strength. It is in contemplation, in gazing at our beloved and longing for him, that we will germinate.

Julian's life and work show that when we do see our smallness and pray her prayer, when we choose Jesus for our heaven, all else will follow. "But seek first his kingdom and his righteousness, and all these things will be given to you as well" (Matthew 6:33).

That giving of our one small self, our tiny beating heart, becomes a spring of living water through which our triune God can bless us and a great many others. This is a wonderful, comforting thing to realize. Julian received an amazing gift which might have stayed a treasure in her head and heart, a small thing to hold onto to give her faith all her days. But because she was willing to give her whole self and life to God through Christ, she does not remain one solitary grain of wheat. Instead, she plants herself, anchors herself, in God. She lays herself down in the dust with him, prostrating herself as all those taking religious vows do, face down in the pigsty of our world. She and her hazelnut sprout there, in the dark of a tiny cell against a church, a "nobody" and her vision of a small nut becomes the beginning of her glorious book, a heart full of passion, a great tree where all the birds of the air might come and learn about our "true rest" in God. A Beautiful Gate into God's heart.

We thank you, Lord, for Julian's wisdom, sacrifice, and example, for her love for us, her *evenchristen*. Show us how to emulate her, how to anchor ourselves in your love, comfort ourselves by the gift of contemplation, and bless your dear ones. Amen.

Julian's Prayer

When we have contemplated our smallness along with Julian, and realized what it means, we are propelled to call on God to be our everything. With the soul Julian depicts who has seen all these things to be true, we can pray her believer's prayer:

> "God, in your goodness, give me yourself, for you are enough for me, and I can ask for nothing less to fully worship you; and if I ask for anything less, I will always be lacking, for only in you do I have everything I need."[1]
> Amen.

Acknowledgments

While my first thanks and whole heart always go to God with any project, there are a number of his wonderful children without whom this book would not exist. My darling husband Rowan, who passed on the instruction to create this book and encouraged me throughout its formation, deserves huge thanks. He helped me believe I could do it, read and gave valuable feedback on the first draft, and fueled me with his love and copious amounts of tea. We are always a team.

Love and appreciation always to my parents, Graham and Valerie, for their love and support. I will see you again.

Gratitude to my sisters in the Redbud Writers Guild, who have all made me feel so welcome and supported, with special thanks to Prasanta Verma Anumolu for her guidance and to Margot Starbuck for her helpful editorial suggestions. Huge thanks to the editorial team at Herald Press, especially to Sara Versluis, for her wise and insightful suggestions, as well as her patience and adaptability. She is an absolute delight to work with.

Dr. Rod Wilson and Dr. Sarah Law have both been invaluable in their kind gifts of time and expertise. Their generosity in reading and their clear insights have made this a far better book than it was, and I am deeply grateful. Any errors that remain are mine alone. I also extend my thanks to Sister Elizabeth Ruth Obbard for the fond memories I have of speaking with her a few precious times at Aylesford about creativity, Julian, and Hildegard.

Thanks too to all my family and friends who have supported us or my writing and especially my *anam cara*, Bev Wilson, who despite being on the other side of the world, always blesses me with her constancy, affection, and dear heart.

Suggested Reading

Allchin, A. M., Sister Benedicta Ward SLG, Sister Eileen Mary SLG, and Sister Mary Paul SLG. *Julian of Norwich: Four Studies*. SLG Press, 1st ed. 1973, 3rd ed. 2022.

Delio, Ilia, OSF. *Clare of Assisi: A Heart Full of Love*. Franciscan Media, 2007.

Foster, Richard. *Prayer: Finding the Heart's True Home*. Hodder and Stoughton, 2008.

Hallesby, Ole. *Prayer*. IVP, 1976.

Julian of Norwich, Mother. *Revelations of Divine Love*, 2nd ed. Edited by Halcyon Backhouse and Rhona Pipe. Hodder and Stoughton, 2009.

Laird, Martin. *Into the Silent Land: A Guide to the Christian Practice of Contemplation*. Oxford University Press, 2006.

———. *An Ocean of Light: Contemplation, Transformation, and Liberation*. Oxford University Press, 2018.

———. *A Sunlit Absence: Silence, Awareness, and Contemplation*. Oxford University Press, 2011.

Lawrence, Brother. *The Practice of the Presence of God*.

Lennon, Dennis, Rev. *Turning the Diamond: Exploring George Herbert's Images of Prayer*. SPCK, 2002.

McColman, Carl. *The New Big Book of Christian Mysticism: An Essential Guide to Contemplative Spirituality*. Broadleaf Books, 2023.

Obbard, Elizabeth Ruth, OCD. *Through Julian's Windows: Growing into Wholeness with Julian of Norwich*. Canterbury Press, 2008.

Rohr, Richard. *Everything Belongs: The Gift of Contemplative Prayer*. Crossroad, 2003.

———. *Immortal Diamond: The Search for Our True Self*. SPCK, 2013.

———. *The Naked Now: Learning to See as the Mystics See*. Crossroad, 2009.

Rolf, Veronica Mary. *An Explorer's Guide to Julian of Norwich*. IVP, 2018.

———. *Julian's Gospel: Illuminating the Life and Revelations of Julian of Norwich*. Orbis Books, 2014.

Teresa of Avila. *The Interior Castle*. Dover Thrift Editions: Religion.

———. *The Way of Perfection*. Dover Thrift Editions: Religion.

Thérèse of Lisieux, St. *The Story of a Soul*. Tan Books, 2010.

Upjohn, Sheila. *In Search of Julian of Norwich*. Darton, Longman and Todd, 1989.

Williams, Rowan. *Silence and Honey Cakes: The Wisdom of the Desert*. Lion Books, 2004.

Notes

Chapter 1
1. See Julian of Norwich, *Revelations of Divine Love*, 2nd ed., ed. Halcyon Backhouse and Rhona Pipe (Hodder and Stoughton, 2009), 8. This edition is Hodder Faith Christian Classics. I have also drawn on another version of *Revelations of Divine Love* (henceforth *RoDL*), trans. Grace Harriet Warrack (Methuen & Company, 1907), available at https://en.wikisource.org/wiki/Revelations_of_Divine_Love. These two translations are henceforth cited in short form throughout the notes by their editors or translator for ease of reading.
2. See *RoDL*, ed. Backhouse and Pipe, xxv–xxvi.
3. My rendering of *RoDL*, trans. Warrack, 10–11, chap. 5. "No bigger than a hazelnut" is from *RoDL*, ed. Backhouse and Pipe, 13.
4. Veronica Mary Rolf, *An Explorer's Guide to Julian of Norwich* (IVP, 2018), 49–50.
5. Elizabeth Ruth Obbard, OCD, *Through Julian's Windows: Growing into Wholeness with Julian of Norwich* (Canterbury Press, 2008).

Chapter 2
1. "The Desert Fathers and Mothers retreated to the outskirts of the cities and into the Deserts of Egypt, Syria and Palestine to think through the meaning of such change and to find a different way of being a Christian in the world." Trevor Miller, "Understanding Desert Monasticism," Northumbria Community, last modified August 8, 2013, https://www.northumbriacommunity.org/articles/understanding-desert-monasticism/.
2. Libreria Editrice Vaticana, "Catechism of the Catholic Church," Vatican, last modified February 22, 2023, https://www.vatican.va/archive/ENG0015/__P9N.HTM.
3. "Teresa of Avila, St. Teresa of Jesus, the Book of Her Life," 8, 5 in the *Collected Works of St. Teresa of Avila*, trans. K. Kavanaugh, OCD, and O. Rodriguez, OCD (Institute of Carmelite Studies, 1976), I, 67;

Richard Rohr, "What Is Mysticism?," YouTube video, 2:23, August 11, 2016, https://www.youtube.com/watch?v=q8jvVmJ1baE.
4 Carl McColman, "Understanding How Contemplation and Mysticism Are Different (and Similar)," *Patheos*, last modified January 27, 2019, https://www.patheos.com/blogs/carlmccolman/2019/01/understanding-how-contemplation-and-mysticism-are-different-and-similar/.
5 Veronica Mary Rolf, *An Explorer's Guide to Julian of Norwich* (IVP, 2018), 54.
6 "And let none of you imagine that, because a sister has had such experiences, she is any better than the rest; the Lord leads each of us as He sees we have need. Such experiences, if we use them aright, prepare us to be better servants of God; but sometimes it is the weakest whom God leads by this road; and so there is no ground here either for approval or for condemnation." Teresa of Avila, *Interior Castle* (Dover Publications, 2007), 131.
7 An image I also found in Martin Laird's works. I highly recommend his trilogy on contemplative prayer: *Into the Silent Land*, *A Sunlit Absence*, and *An Ocean of Light*.

Chapter 3
1 *RoDL*, ed. Backhouse and Pipe, 33.
2 *RoDL*, ed. Backhouse and Pipe, 35.
3 Bonaventure, *Bonaventure: The Soul's Journey to God* 1, 14, trans. Ewert Cousins (Paulist Press, 1978), 100.
4 From the poem "Prayer" by George Herbert, as quoted by Dennis Lennon, *Turning the Diamond: Exploring George Herbert's Images of Prayer* (SPCK, 2002).
5 Lennon, 2.
6 Veronica Mary Rolf, *Julian's Gospel: Illuminating the Life and Revelations of Julian of Norwich* (Orbis, 2014), 280.
7 Rolf, 196.
8 See *RoDL*, ed. Backhouse and Pipe, 60.
9 Ilia Delio, OSF, *Clare of Assisi: A Heart Full of Love* (Franciscan Media, 2007), 54.
10 Delio, 54.
11 My rendering of *RoDL*, trans. Warrack, 10–11, chap. 5.
12 Rolf, *Julian's Gospel*, 275.
13 Veronica Rolf, "Julian and the Hazelnut," *Julian's Voice* (blog), July 31, 2021, https://www.juliansvoice.com/veronicas-blog/julian-and-the-hazelnut.

Chapter 4
1 Veronica Mary Rolf, *Julian's Gospel: Illuminating the Life and Revelations of Julian of Norwich* (Orbis, 2014), 275.
2 "The Pale Blue Dot" is a photograph of Earth taken February 14,

1990, by NASA's *Voyager 1* at a distance of 3.7 billion miles (6 billion kilometers) from the sun. The image inspired the title of scientist Carl Sagan's book *Pale Blue Dot: A Vision of the Human Future in Space*, in which he writes, "Look again at that dot. That's here. That's home. That's us." NASA, February 5, 2019, https://science.nasa.gov/resource/voyager-1s-pale-blue-dot/.
3. Rolf, *Julian's Gospel*, 275.
4. *RoDL*, ed. Backhouse and Pipe, 20.
5. *RoDL*, ed. Backhouse and Pipe, 12.
6. Saint Louis-Marie de Montfort, *The True Devotion to the Blessed Virgin* (Baronius Press, 2006), 2.
7. De Montfort, 7.

Chapter 5

1. "*Saint Clare of Montefalco Receiving the Cross in Her Heart*," Feminae: Medieval Women and Gender Index, accessed April 22, 2024, https://inpress.lib.uiowa.edu/feminae/DetailsPage.aspx?Feminae_ID=31984.
2. *RoDL*, ed. Backhouse and Pipe, 122.
3. See Teresa of Avila, *Interior Castle* (Dover Publications, 2007), 70–72.
4. *RoDL*, ed. Backhouse and Pipe, 28.
5. Veronica Mary Rolf, *Julian's Gospel: Illuminating the Life and Revelations of Julian of Norwich* (Orbis, 2014), 274.
6. *RoDL*, ed. Backhouse and Pipe, 57.
7. See *RoDL*, ed. Backhouse and Pipe, 56.
8. *RoDL*, ed. Backhouse and Pipe, 121.
9. Thomas Merton, *Conjectures of a Guilty Bystander* (Bantam, 1994), 153–54.
10. My rendering of *RoDL*, trans. Warrack.
11. In Julian's vision, Jesus has yet to have the blood and water let out of his side, which happens after his death. "One of the soldiers pierced Jesus' side with a spear, bringing a sudden flow of blood and water" (John 19:34).
12. *RoDL*, ed. Backhouse and Pipe, 63.
13. *RoDL*, ed. Backhouse and Pipe, 59–60.
14. Thérèse of Lisieux, *The Story of a Soul* (Tan Books, 2010), 147.
15. Sheila Upjohn, *In Search of Julian of Norwich* (Darton, Longman and Todd, 1989), 21n.
16. Upjohn, 22.
17. See *RoDL*, ed. Backhouse and Pipe, 19–20.
18. Corrie ten Boom with John Sherrill and Elisabeth Sherrill, *The Hiding Place* (World Wide Publications, 1971), 159.
19. Elizabeth Ruth Obbard, OCD, *Through Julian's Windows* (Canterbury Press, 2008), xii.
20. All short quotes here and to the end of the chapter are from my rendering of *RoDL*, trans. Warrack.

Chapter 6

1 "As it happens, the earliest extant reference to the Earth being a globe comes from 200 years after Pythagoras was born, in a dialogue by Plato (427–347 BC) called the *Phaedo* (108e). While Plato didn't invent the idea, it's clear from his remarks that it was a novel and inchoate concept at the time. On that basis, we should date the genesis of the spherical earth to the early 4th century BC." James, Hannam, "Who First Realised the Earth Was Round?," *Antigone*, last modified September 10, 2023, https://antigonejournal.com/2023/09/ancient-greeks-earth-round/.

2 The first recorded, unambiguous European references to a spherical Earth are found in the work of ancient Greek philosophers, such as Plato and Aristotle. By the time the Roman writer Pliny the Elder was writing the first part of his *Natural History* around CE 77, the fact that the Earth is a sphere was treated as common knowledge: "We all agree on the earth's shape. For surely we always speak of the round ball of the Earth." Pliny, *Natural History*, II.64. These views continued into the medieval period, since even the changing hours of daylight throughout the year made it evident that the Earth was round.

Around 723 or 725, the monk Bede explained to his students: "The reason why the same days are of unequal length is the roundness of the Earth, for not without reason is it called 'the orb of the world' on the pages of Holy Scripture and of ordinary literature. It is, in fact, a sphere set in the middle of the whole universe. It is not merely circular like a shield [or] spread out like a wheel, but resembles more a ball, being equally round in all directions." Bede, *The Reckoning of Time*, trans. Faith Wallis (Liverpool University Press, 1999), 91. Quoted in Alison Hudson, "'The Earth Is, in Fact, Round,'" British Library *Medieval Manuscripts Blog*, May 24, 2018, https://blogs.bl.uk/digitisedmanuscripts/2018/05/the-earth-is-in-fact-round.html.

3 "Saint Benedict urged his monks to pray all 150 Psalms in a week, noting that the Desert Fathers often strenuously recited all 150 each day." "The Rosary and the Liturgy," Monastery of the Holy Cross, August 12, 2015, https://chicagomonk.org/about/the-priors-blog/the-rosary-and-the-liturgy/.

4 See *RoDL*, ed. Backhouse and Pipe, 188.

5 Sheila Upjohn, *In Search of Julian of Norwich* (Darton, Longman and Todd, 1989), 52.

6 Upjohn, 53, quoting *RoDL,* chap. 60.

7 *RoDL*, ed. Backhouse and Pipe, 158.

8 *RoDL*, ed. Backhouse and Pipe, 73.

9 Eliza Stiles, "Precious Food of True Life": Christ Our Mother, Female Embodiment and the Eucharist in Julian of Norwich's *Revelations of Divine Love*," *Priscilla Papers* 34, no. 1 (Winter 2020). Used with kind permission.

10 *RoDL*, ed. Backhouse and Pipe, 166–67.
11 See *RoDL*, ed. Backhouse and Pipe, 17.
12 Bonaventure, *Bonaventure: The Soul's Journey to God* 1, 14, trans. Ewert Cousins (Paulist Press, 1978), 100.

Chapter 7
1 My rendering of *RoDL*, trans. Warrack.
2 Ilia Delio, OSF, *Clare of Assisi: A Heart Full of Love* (Franciscan Media, 2007), 51.
3 Delio, 109.

Chapter 8
1 *RoDL*, ed. Backhouse and Pipe, 122.
2 *RoDL*, ed. Backhouse and Pipe, 138.
3 *RoDL*, ed. Backhouse and Pipe, 107.
4 *RoDL*, ed. Backhouse and Pipe, 106.
5 *RoDL*, ed. Backhouse and Pipe, 99.
6 Veronica Rolf, *An Explorer's Guide to Julian of Norwich* (IVP, 2018), 37.
7 Rolf, 44.
8 Saint Augustine, *Confessions*, Book 1.
9 My rendering of *RoDL*, trans. Warrack.
10 My rendering of *RoDL*, trans. Warrack.
11 Rolf, *Guide to Julian of Norwich*, 49.
12 Rolf, 51.
13 The Order of Julian of Norwich was founded in 1985. You can find their website at https://www.orderofjulian.org.
14 "The brief poem-prayer [Nada te turbe] commonly known today as the Bookmark of St. Teresa or St. Teresa's Bookmark, was found on a prayer card in her breviary (Liturgy of the Hours or Divine Office book)." Bookmark of Saint Teresa of Avila," April 22, 2024, https://www.knightsoftheholyeucharist.com/bookmark-of-saint-teresa-of-avila-prayer-download.
15 My rendering of *RoDL*, trans. Warrack.
16 *RoDL*, ed. Backhouse and Pipe, 121.
17 Liz Carter, *Valuable: Why Your Worth Is Not Defined by How Useful You Feel* (Good Book Company, 2023).
18 My rendering of *RoDL*, trans. Warrack.

Chapter 9
1 My rendering of *RoDL*, trans. Warrack.
2 *RoDL*, ed. Backhouse and Pipe, 215.
3 *RoDL*, ed. Backhouse and Pipe, 138, 111.
4 My rendering of *RoDL*, trans. Warrack.
5 *RoDL*, ed. Backhouse and Pipe, 63.
6 *RoDL*, ed. Backhouse and Pipe, 64.

Chapter 10
1. Mark Oakley, *The Splash of Words: Believing in Poetry* (Canterbury Press, 2016).
2. *RoDL*, ed. Backhouse and Pipe, 122.
3. My rendering of *RoDL*, trans. Warrack, 35–36, chap. 15.
4. My rendering of *RoDL*, trans. Warrack trans.
5. *RoDL*, ed. Backhouse and Pipe, 62.

Chapter 11
1. My rendering of *RoDL*, trans. Warrack, 27, chap. 11.
2. *RoDL*, ed. Backhouse and Pipe, 159.
3. *RoDL*, ed. Backhouse and Pipe, 158.
4. My rendering of *RoDL*, trans. Warrack, 144, chap. 58.

Chapter 12
1. My rendering of *RoDL*, trans. Warrack.
2. *RoDL*, ed. Backhouse and Pipe, 67.
3. *RoDL*, ed. Backhouse and Pipe, 123.
4. *RoDL*, ed. Backhouse and Pipe, 100.
5. Sister Eileen Mary, SLG, Sister Mary Paul, SLG, Sister Benedicta Ward, and A. M. Allchin, *Julian of Norwich: Four Studies Sixth Centenary of the* Revelations of Divine Love (SLG Press, 2022), 16. First published 1973.
6. *RoDL*, ed. Backhouse and Pipe, 44.
7. *RoDL*, ed. Backhouse and Pipe, 17.
8. My rendering of *RoDL*, trans. Warrack, 102, chap. 48.
9. *RoDL*, ed. Backhouse and Pipe, 90.
10. My rendering of *RoDL*, trans. Warrack.
11. *RoDL*, ed. Backhouse and Pipe, 149.
12. *RoDL*, ed. Backhouse and Pipe, 215.
13. My rendering of *RoDL*, trans. Warrack, 202–3, chap. 86.

Conclusion
1. *RoDL*, ed. Backhouse and Pipe, 90.

Julian's Prayer
1. My rendering of *RoDL*, trans. Warrack.

The Author

Keren Dibbens-Wyatt is a writer and artist with a passion for prayer, poetry, story, and color. She is a Christian contemplative who writes to encourage and entertain readers of all ages. Keren is the author of numerous books, and her work also features regularly in literary journals and anthologies. She lives in southeast England with her husband and is housebound due to chronic illness.